PRAISE FOR *SOME GAVE IT ALL*

Go inside the Marine missions in the Vietnam War like never told before. Jaw dropping action in incomprehensible conditions. Danny Lane and I were both young warriors when we participated in the historic Operation Meade River in 1968. An operation that took 20 days to knock out the North Vietnamese Army stronghold in Dodge City, but knock it out we did! A grunt Marine is the most dangerous fighting machine in the world. Marines are always the first in and the last out. As long as there are Marines, America will be safe. God Bless the 14,844 Marines that gave it all in the abyss of Vietnam. *Some Gave it All* is a must read for every red-blooded American!

Colonel Phil Torres
U. S. Marine Corps (Ret.), Vietnam Veteran,
Silver Star Medal Recipient during Operation Meade River

Danny Lane is an American warrior in both war and peace. *Some Gave It All* is a must-read for anyone who wants the real skinny on the brotherhood of combat. Civilians, as well as veterans, will find themselves mesmerized and brought into the action like never before.

John Ligato
Vietnam Combat Marine (Survivor of Hue, 3 Purple Hearts),
Retired FBI Special Agent,
Author of the John Booker Series

This is an amazing story of courage and sacrifice. I'm almost at a loss for words. Every God-fearing American ought to read this. It'll get your heart pounding, and you'll be forever grateful for the men and women who keep this country safe, including American hero Danny Lane. I am proud to have him on my staff as a combat tactics instructor.

Jason Hanson
Former CIA Officer, author of the *New York Times* Bestseller *Spy Secrets that Can Save Your Life*

Danny, the legacy of the Marine Corps is enriched future by what you have written, but more importantly, by what you did for this great nation. As a Marine, I thank you for your story and your great service to our country. I admire how you stood the faith in God, the Marine Corps, and America during the most agonizing and painful times that no one would ever want to endure. The more I read, the better the storyline went, and the more immersed I became.

Colonel Steven B. Vitali
USMC (Ret.)

Some Gave It All is a brutally powerful, inspiring depiction of the sacrifice, honor, and faith of a young Marine in the abyss of the Vietnam War. It reads like an action movie I would love to direct.

Art Camacho
Award Winning Motion Picture Director

Some Gave It All is a stirring story of service in Vietnam by a United States Marine who is dealing with post-traumatic stress disorder following the war. It is extremely well-written and does a tremendous job of balancing the action of war with the human interest aspect of coping with horrors of war. The book captures the reader's attention from the opening sentence and holds it throughout the entire book. As a former enlisted Marine and current Army Lt. Colonel, I enjoyed the battle action as well as the insight into the military strategy that was aptly depicted in the book. As a physician, I was captivated by the post-war story of a hero dealing with PTSD and coping with the horrors he had seen 40 years prior. *Some Gave It All* is a fitting tribute to America's "forgotten war" and to those that served who will never forget it.

Colonel Scott M. Hovis
Lt. Colonel, US Army MD

As I read Danny's story in *Some Gave It All* it made me feel as though I could see what Danny was seeing. Danny was one of the lucky ones making it home, but it is obvious that his sacrifice was tremendous and something was left in the jungle. Thank you for telling your story — no doubt it will help shed light on the reality that is war. Danny Lane is a true American Warrior and hero.

Robert Mclean
Federal Air Marshal

Through the fire of the Vietnam War, Danny Lane became a leader. He has always pushed beyond the limits of greatness his whole life. *Some Gave It All* reminds us of the courage and sacrifice our young men and women make for our country. Danny's incredible story of war and the aftermath should be read by all veterans of all wars. I felt like I was in the action from the first page through the end. What a read!

Bill Hall
Retired Federal Air Marshal, Former World Rated
Kickboxer, author of *Predator Group*

Heroism is complicated. *Some Gave It All* looks at several perspectives; from inside the soul of those who serve and the lives that are affected by their actions. Mark Bowser and Danny Lane paint a picture with their style and word selection that draws you into the changes and feelings of all. There is something there for each of us to learn from.

Julie Ann Sullivan
Speaker, Trainer, Podcaster

I just finished reading *Some Gave It All* yesterday. I was truly moved by Danny's storytelling — it hurled me back in time and was very emotional. It was very well written, and I couldn't put it down until I finished! His story showed so much compassion and struggle within himself for all around him, whether friend or enemy. Danny, I appreciate your courage, your love of country and your love for your fellow soldiers, especially your love and caring for my husband, Sotere.

Sophia Karas

Some Gave It All shows the horror of war and the emotional toll and recovery of a real American hero, Danny Lane. Without brave Marines like Danny Lane, we would not be free. After reading this book, I will never forget that.

Lee Cockerell
Executive Vice President,
Walt Disney World®Resort (Ret.) and bestselling author of
Creating Magic, The Customer Rules,
Time Management Magic and *Career Magic*

Some Gave It All keeps you on the edge of your seat! The action is non-stop and Danny's struggle to survive is gripping and intense. Danny was a hell of a cop. I loved working with him and knew when going through a door together; he always had my back.

Richard Kemp
ATF Resident in Charge,
Special Federal Agent (Ret.)

So many of us have never had to experience the horrors of war or the hurdles of returning to a normal life afterward. This really gave me new appreciation for the sacrifices these soldiers made for us. Danny's story of his combat in Vietnam is told in visceral, gripping detail with moment-to-moment suspense. Mark Bowser narrative keeps you guessing as he bounces between modern day and wartime, even throwing some twists at you that you won't expect.

Cory Edwards
Writer / Director of *Hoodwinked*

A great story that I can relate to. As a retired US Marine of 20 years, after two combat tours in Iraq (Fallujah and Rahmadi) and Afghanistan, I too have been there — walking through hell during the day and dancing with the devil at night. Wondering every day if the enemy has your number. Seeing your brothers getting wasted by sniper fire and then having it escalate into a complex attack. Love the book! Semper Fi!

Staff Sergeant James Nunguesser
Decorated USMC combat veteran (Ret.)

Danny Lane and Mark Bowser have written an exciting roller coaster of an adventure. The amazing thing is that it is a true story. *Some Gave It All* grabbed me from the first paragraph and wouldn't let go until the last word.

Pat Williams
Orlando Magic senior vice president,
Author of *The Success Intersection*

SOME
GAVE IT ALL

Through the Fire of the Vietnam War

Danny Lane
&
Mark Bowser

Made for Success
PUBLISHING

Made for Success Publishing
P.O. Box 1775
Issaquah, WA 98027

If you are seeking to purchase this book in quantity for sales promotion or corporate use, please contact Made for Success at 425-657-0300 or email Sales@MadeforSuccess.net. Your local bookstore can also help you with discounted bulk purchase options.

Library of Congress Cataloging-in-Publication data

Lane, Danny and Bowser, Mark: Some Gave it All: Through the Fire of the Vietnam War / Danny Lane, Mark Bowser Seattle, WA : Made for Success Pub., 2018.
pages cm

ISBN: 9781613398265 (alk. paper)
LCCN: 2017905986

1. Biographies & Memoirs > Leaders & Notable People > Military > Vietnam War
2. History > Military > United States > Vietnam War
3. History > Americas > United States > Military History > Veterans
4. History > Asia

Printed in the United States of America

TABLE OF CONTENTS

DEDICATION

I dedicate this book to the 14,844 Marines that "Gave it All" through the fire of Vietnam and the 88,000 plus that were wounded. Specifically, the Marines in 3rd Battalion Fifth Marines that fought beside me in the abyss of hell. It takes a special kind of warrior that is willing to sacrifice their lives for the freedom of all Americans. Thank God for these American Warriors.

Danny Lane

I dedicate this book to my wonderful wife, Sarah. You are truly a gift from God. We have been together through the storms of life as well as the sunset beaches of joy. You are the love of my life and I look forward to walking the future with you.

I also dedicate this to our children Andrew, Hannah, and Rebecca. You are a blessing to us. We are proud of you and smile with joy on the marks you are making on the world.

Mark Bowser

ACKNOWLEDGMENTS

First, I have to thank God. Without Him by my side, I surely would have perished. I could feel His presence with me in the heat of battle; He always showed up right on time and took me through the fire of the storm. When so many other Marines fell within inches of me, I was still alive, fighting back. Even wounded, He wouldn't let me leave the battlefield. It was my purpose in life to continue to fight for the American cause and survive the war.

To Sotere Karas (The Greek), a nineteen-year-old kid from Cleveland whose parents came to the USA from Greece: You are undoubtedly the bravest and coolest person in combat I have ever seen. You always smiled in the face of death.

To Virgil Wells from Arkansas, Nick Yankanich from Philly, and all the Marines in my Squad: this book is to tell our story and honor all of you that fought beside me.

To my beautiful, loving and understanding wife, Gina: I want to sincerely thank you. You felt the pain I still had inside after forty years. You encouraged me to write this story to help others understand what I went through, and to help me find peace within myself. You comforted me when you saw the tears coming down my face while I was writing this story. You know He has another purpose for me. I love you with all of my heart.

A special dedication to my co-writer Mark Bowser: It was no accident that we met. God brought you into my life to get this story told. You are a special man. Mark has spent a long two years putting my words onto the pages.

Special thanks to Bryan Heathman, Dee Heathman, and the rest of the staff at Made for Success Publishing. Thank you for taking a chance on me and telling **our** story. It has been a dream working with all of you.

A BIG shout out to the great people that read advanced copies of *Some Gave it All* and supported this project with their encouragements and endorsements: Colonel Steve Vitali, USMC (retired); Colonel Phil Torres, USMC (retired); Pat Williams (Orlando Magic Senior Vice President); John Ligato (retired FBI Agent, Vietnam Combat Marine and Author); Jason Hanson (former CIA Officer, Author and creator of *Spy Secrets & Spy Combatives*); Lee Cockerell (Executive Vice President — Retired and Inspired — of Walt Disney World® Resort and the author of *Creating Magic*); Lt. Colonel Scott M. Hovis (US Army); Robert Mclean (Federal Air Marshal); Bill Hall (Retired Federal Air Marshal); Julie Ann Sullivan (Speaker & Trainer); Sophia Karas (wife of the Greek); Art Camacho (Motion Picture Director); Keith Vitali (Martial Arts World Champion); Ron Heller (USMC Vietnam Marine); Richard Kemp (ATF Federal Agent, retired) and many others.

PROLOGUE

"**B**ROKEN ARROW! BROKEN ARROW!" BELLOWED A soldier into his field radio. "Command . . . Command . . . we are being overrun!" The soldier put away the radio and began firing his machine gun. Explosions dimly lit the night sky like fireworks on the Fourth of July. In a nearby foxhole, a young Marine saw the shadowy, ghost-like silhouettes of the suicidal enemy sappers as they charged through the American defenses. The North Vietnamese Army used these demolition commandos expertly to breach the American defenses. Terror filled the bones of the young Marine. A kamikaze sapper charged his position, wired with explosives, leaving him little time to ponder his feelings. The sapper jumped into the foxhole, landing on top of the young Marine. The two men struggled hand-to-hand in a fierce battle to the death. The young Marine knew he had only seconds before the sapper would activate his explosives, killing both men.

With a swift, desperate motion, the young Marine swept his bayonet from its sheath and drove it into the waiting chest of the enemy. Silence enveloped the young Marine's soul. At that moment, it was as if all life had stopped. The young Marine looked into the dying eyes of the enemy, then watched as his chest heaved with its final breath. But it was those piercing eyes that haunted the young Marine at that moment — and for every moment to come.

LATE SEPTEMBER in West Virginia was normally cold and crisp. This year, 2006, was no different. As the hazy fog began to roll in over the hills, the frail man in his mid-fifties staggered to his feet. He was wearing only a pair of black shorts that hung on his emaciated frame. Hard gravel crunched under his feet, then a wooden beam, then more gravel, then another beam. He walked on the tracks as the whistle grew closer. The Amtrak train had arrived right on schedule.

He collapsed on the gravel beside the railroad tracks. Startled by the blaring siren of the fast approaching Amtrack train, he labored to open his eyes and was blinded by the oncoming light of the locomotive.

He lifted his head in the approaching light and water dripped off his head and hair. A drop landed in his right eye, and the man slowly wiped it away. He then closed his eyes as if to entrust his fate to the oncoming train. At that moment, a nearby drunkard staggered forward and shoved the man hard off the railroad tracks, narrowly saving his life. As the train passed, the man struggled back to his feet. The drunkard angrily slurred, "Man, what the h*ll is wrrrong with yyou! You tryin' to kill yyourself?"

The man's eyes wandered and tried to focus on the blurred image of the Kroger Supermarket in the near distance. Struggling towards the parking lot, he stumbled through the automatic door, and into the brightly-lit grocery store. The man needed help — and he wanted help. But no words came from his mouth. Finally, he was overcome with weakness and fell, his head hitting hard on the concrete floor.

A Kroger cashier looked over the counter and shook her head in disgust. "Just another drunk," she thought to herself. She picked up the phone and dialed 911.

"911, what is your emergency?"

"This is Brenda over at the Kroger store on First Street. We have another drunk passed out on the floor. No shoes and no shirt. He's unconscious."

The man struggled to form the words he needed but was only able to quietly whisper, "Daniel Edward Lane, United States Marine Corps, number 2461294." No one heard.

The police and EMS arrived together just a few minutes after the 911 call. They did a quick examination and quickly lifted the man on a gurney and into the ambulance. He appeared intoxicated, but there was something about him — something different.

As the ambulance sped to the hospital, EMS called into dispatch. "Unit 410 running code to St. Mary's . . . white male mid-fifties, unconscious, no ID, possible concussion, vitals are not good. Call ahead to have the trauma unit on standby."

"10-4, 410. I will notify them," came the immediate response from dispatch.

The driver stomped hard on the gas pedal. He had the feeling that time was a commodity they were running short of if the guy was going to survive.

On arrival at the hospital, EMS hurriedly pushed the gurney through the large glass sliding doors and into the ER. Dr. Shane Bowen moved hastily to the door as soon as he heard the ambulance pull up. "Who do we have here?"

"Don't know, Doc. No ID. He just walked into the Kroger and collapsed. Possible concussion. He has a knot on the back of his head. His vitals aren't good."

"Ok. Let's get him into the room, stat. Get that IV hooked up, and let's run his vitals again," said Dr. Bowen.

After a few minutes, the man was hooked up to an EKG machine, with an IV running from his arm to a bag of clear liquid on a pole next to the bed. Dr. Bowen scratched his head. Who was this mystery man, and what was going on in his body? Dr. Bowen looked towards the police officer standing nearby and asked, "Do you have any information on this guy yet?"

"No. Not really," said the officer. "He was seen on the railroad tracks, acting like he didn't care if he lived or died. He was pushed out of the way of the Amtrak just before it hit him. There are no missing persons reported matching his description. So far, no one has called in with any additional information."

"Wow, that drunkard must have been his guardian angel," said Dr. Bowen. He then turned to his medical assistants who were waiting near the bed. "Let's get him to X-Ray to get his head looked at, and then let's get him upstairs."

The door buzzed and someone hurriedly entered the room. Dr. Bowen instinctively turned to see who had entered. To his surprise, it wasn't a nurse. A young man in his mid-twenties entered the room with a look of despair. The strong, fit young man located his father and ran to his side.

"May I help you?" asked Dr. Bowen.

"That's my Dad. I have been looking for him all night. He disappeared, and I couldn't find him. I finally called the police department, and they told me that an unconscious man had been picked up at the Kroger and brought here. I'm Chris Lane."

"Yes. He came in that way and is still in serious condition. What is his name?"

"Danny . . . Danny Lane," said Chris.

"Danny Lane, the police officer and karate guy?" asked a shocked Dr. Bowen. "The one who knows Chuck Norris and brought him to town?"

"Yeah, that's him," said Chris.

"I thought he looked familiar. I remember seeing him on the news. But he's lost a lot of weight. This is Danny Lane?"

"Yeah. That's him. Is he going to be alright? He has been really sick for the past five months. He's been having flashbacks from the war and talking out of his head," said Chris.

"What war was he in?" Dr. Bowen asked.

"Vietnam. He was a Marine and saw a lot of combat."

"Wow! He must have gone through h*ll. That had to be about . . . forty years ago! What years was he in Vietnam?" asked Dr. Bowen.

"Nineteen sixty-eight and nineteen sixty-nine."

THE SOUND was deafening in its silence. It's not that he was alone — there were many people within a few feet of him. There were even massive, multi-propellered helicopters in the near distance being prepared for liftoff. But, it was the loneliness of his thoughts. "What have I gotten myself into?" thought nineteen-year-old Danny Lane. Just two days ago he was stateside, and now he was in Vietnam. He adjusted his helmet to sit more snugly over his short, brown hair. It was November 20, 1968, and Danny and his fellow Marines sat on the cold, wet tarmac in full combat gear.

It was 4:00 AM, and it was cool. It was not only cool, but it was wet; the monsoon season was in full swing. During this period, rainfall averaged an inch a day — an everlasting reality that Danny would soon learn to ignore. But on this given day and at this given moment, he was an inexperienced "boot." You could tell a boot apart from everyone else. For one thing, their green, camouflaged, perfectly-creased uniforms and shiny boots looked like they had just come off a store shelf. Danny couldn't even be called a "grunt" yet. A grunt was a new soldier who had at least *seen* combat. A grunt was given a little bit of respect — but just a little. A boot? None. No one wanted to be next to a boot. Boots were untested, and no one wanted to be next to them when the bullets started flying.

The helicopters fired up their engines, and the Marines started moving slowly across the dimly-lit tarmac towards the choppers. It was raining pretty hard now, and Danny could hardly see where he was going. Right beside him walked his best friend, Sotere Karas, who was also nineteen years old.

Sotere was small in stature, but large in heart. He had tremendous courage and always had a smile on his face. Danny and Sotere had met in boot camp at Parris Island, SC, and had become fast friends. Sotere became known as "the Greek," because he always carried the Greek flag with him, which he planted in the moist Vietnamese ground in the heat of battle. Sotere was the son of Greek immigrants and still held citizenship in Greece. He had only been an American citizen a short time before he joined the Marine Corps.

On this very early morning in Southeast Asia, Danny and Sotere each wore one-hundred-pound backpacks, which were getting heavier by the minute because of the soaking rain. Danny and Sotere climbed aboard one of the helicopters along with the rest of their squad. In all, there were thirteen of them: twelve Marines and their Squad Leader, Corporal Kessler.

Kessler was a slim man with a harshness in his features that reminded one of a constipated pit bull. He had what was known as a "thousand-yard stare," and there was no doubt that he was in charge. In his nine months in the country, Kessler had seen his share of action and had survived many battles.

The big bird lifted off and joined the formation of choppers headed toward the war zone. Operation Meade River was about to commence. It was to become the largest helicopter assault of the entire war. Five thousand Marines were involved in the operation. The North Vietnamese Army and the Viet Cong had embedded themselves in a place the Americans called Dodge City, known for the shoot-'em-up, gunslinger style of fighting that took place there.

As Danny and Sotere tried to collect their courage, one of the experienced gunners looked at them and said, "You boots had better sit your butts on your helmets."

"Why?" asked a bewildered Sotere.

"Because bullets can come up right through this flimsy piece of crap we call a helicopter hull and go straight up your a**."

Danny and Sotere immediately jerked their helmets off their heads and perched upon them. The battle-hardened Marine who had given the boys this sage advice just shook his head with a knowing smile and muttered, "Boots. You can't live with them, and we aren't supposed to shoot them." He and all the other experienced Marines on board roared in laughter. Danny glanced uneasily over at Sotere. They were beginning to hate this place already.

They had been flying for what seemed forever, even though Dodge City was only a short 20 miles away. The unknown can be a very scary place, but flying into it while knowing the worst is yet to come can be downright terrifying. Time seemed to slow to a crawl on board that helicopter, at least for Danny and Sotere.

Not so far below, the battle had already begun. Explosions and gunfire rocked the ground. As their helicopter began its descent toward the Landing Zone (LZ), an explosion was heard and immediately the helicopter shuddered. Danny and Sotere looked nervously at each other. What had happened? They didn't have to wait long for the answer.

"Chopper up front is hit. She is going down!" the pilot screamed.

An enemy rocket had just penetrated the hull of the helicopter directly in front of theirs. The chopper hit the jungle canopy below and burst into flames. Death hovered above the crash. How many Marines had just been snuffed out? Danny didn't know at the time. A whole squad for sure — maybe more.

"We're drawing fire!" the gunner screamed. "Hold on to something!" As bullets riddled the hull of the helicopter, Danny quickly grabbed hold of a hand brace attached to the left side of the craft.

The pilot banked sharply left and accelerated to full throttle in an attempt to get out of the kill zone. Sotere lost his balance and fell off of his helmet. He quickly sat back upon it and hung on with everything he had in him. As all of this was going on, the helicopter gunner began firing his huge M-60 machine gun out of the gun port, an opening near the front of the aircraft. Danny and Sotere's knuckles were snow white from the death grip they each had on their respective hand grips inside the Boeing-Vertol CH-46 Sea Knight helicopter.

The helicopter was being buffeted from all sides like an abandoned leaf in a hail storm on a mid-summer eve. But this was no summer storm. This was the Viet Cong raining gunfire upon them. Looking out the tiny windows of the CH-46, Danny and Sotere saw explosions not so far below. The sound of the gunfire in their ears was petrifying. Danny glanced over at Sotere. His face said it all: pure terror. The same face Danny knew he wore if he could only see himself in a mirror.

The CH-46 banked hard again, this time to the right, and sped away from the hostile fire. They had traveled a few hundred yards in a matter of seconds. The door gunner looked back at the Marines and yelled, "Get ready to disembark!" With that, all the Marines got to their feet. Danny and Sotere followed suit.

Just then, the aircraft was rocked again from the bombardment of gunfire. As the ramp at the rear of the chopper opened, the door gunner yelled: "Jump! Now! Get out . . . NOW!"

As the Marines launched themselves out of the helicopter, the door gunner started raining his own fire down again on the enemy position. Bursts of light filled the air. Some of it was from the rear gunner's own tracer bullets; much of it was from the enemy's ammunition which was now riddling the hull of the American helicopter.

Not knowing how high the helicopter was off the ground, Danny somehow managed to muster up the courage to leap into the unknown air. He figured it had to be safer on the ground — at least; he hoped it was. He jumped into the dead of night, and into the seeking grip of the enemy.

It seemed like forever before Danny hit the ground. When he finally did, he hit hard. His body shuddered from the shock of the impact as he rolled over onto his side. He slowly began to get to his feet as Sotere landed right behind him.

They were greeted with more hostile fire, and they immediately scuttled off into the cover of the dark jungle. Foliage bristled under the assault as they ran and dove into the brush. Welcome to Vietnam.

CHAPTER ONE

OPERATION MEADE RIVER: AT THE GATES OF HADES

RUNNING THROUGH THE VIETNAM JUNGLE after leaping from the back of their helicopter, Danny and Sotere were met with a harsh reality; They were alone and had been left behind, separated from their squad. Taking enemy fire as soon as they hit the ground, they hustled into the jungle for cover.

How did that happen? It wasn't done on purpose — It was dark, and enemy fire was everywhere. Those few seconds of separation between soldiers jumping out of a moving helicopter had spread the squad out further than planned.

When they hit the ground, cover was of the utmost importance. Survival depended on it. So, they hit the ground and spread out like a hand with its fingers outstretched. It was a miracle that Danny and Sotere hadn't been separated from each other.

There they were, in a dark, dense jungle in Southeast Asia. The enemy was all around them. What should they do? What could they do? In such moments, all your weary mind and body can lean on are your faith, training, and discipline.

Can you hear it? The rustle of the enemy walking about two yards from your left ear? If they discover you, you're dead; and not a very pleasant death. That is what Danny and Sotere were going through on that first night November 20th, 1968, in the bush. In the distance, they could hear the battle raging on at the site of the downed helicopter. Their fellow Marines were attempting a rescue of any possible survivors. Americans, and particularly Marines, don't leave a fellow Marine behind.

However, Danny and Sotere were in no position to help their fellow Marines. In fact, they kind of felt left behind themselves. The only protection they had were a few blades of grass and a few twigs. The enemy also outnumbered them. So, what should they do? What would *you* do?

As he lay flat on his belly, Danny thought back to his boot camp days at Parris Island, SC. Gunnery Plummer had always told them that you never know what part of training may be the one thing to save your life. But you will know that one thing when it happens.

Without a doubt in his mind, Danny knew what part of training was saving him now. Every day after chowing at Parris Island, the drill instructors would take their men and make them stand at attention outside in the sticky, hot South Carolina sun in order to allow the sand fleas to chew on the troops. The drill instructors said, "You all ate. Now, it is their turn."

The sand fleas would climb up Danny's nose, in his ears, and in every other place, you don't want an insect to crawl up and bite. If the fresh soldiers swatted at the annoying bugs or moved to avoid them, that was it, next was a six-foot grave because they had just given away their position. Danny and his fellow Marines learned quickly how to not move a muscle under the most uncomfortable circumstances.

A little overkill, you think? That is what Danny thought too until he was surrounded by the Viet Cong and North Vietnamese Army who were determined to find him and kill him. At that moment, Danny was thankful for the sand fleas. Those little annoying insects gave him the foundation for tremendous mental, emotional, and physical discipline — discipline that might just save his life.

But, at that moment, fear was the dominating element for these two young men. "What are we gonna do now, Danny?" Sotere whispered.

"How am I supposed to know, Greek?" Danny responded.

"We're screwed! That's what it is!"

"No one told us crap . . . where to go or what to do." Danny whispers.

Sotere, still whispering: "Well . . . we got to do something."

"No sh** Greek! Let's just lay low until daylight, and then maybe we will be able to figure something out," said Danny.

Sotere sighed, and then a small smile crept onto the corners of his mouth. "Well, at least we got to see the world." Despite the situation, Danny couldn't stop a smile from forming on his own face. The Greek always had the uncanny ability to add some light in the darkest of dark places.

The night sky seemed to hang on for eternity. Ever so slowly, daylight began its upward climb in the east. Finally, the blades of jungle foliage began to lighten around them as sunbeams graced their surfaces. The air was rancid with the smell of gunpowder and fuel from the downed chopper. Danny and Sotere were still flat on their bellies, a position they had maintained for what felt like forever. Danny glanced over at Sotere and asked, "Greek, you ready to move out?"

Sotere sighed deeply and said, "Yeah, let's do it. I didn't enlist to die out here like a wild boar. I joined the Marines to kick some a**."

Sotere stretched out his arm and pulled his backpack close to him. He opened it and began rummaging through the contents. In a moment, he pulled out an Instamatic camera and wound the crank on the top of the device. He then pointed it at Danny and snapped a close-up picture.

"What the h*ll?" asked Danny.

Sotere flashed a grin and said, "Just documenting the moment."

"What, a Kodak moment?" asked Danny, with a grin on his own face now.

"Yeah. Now we can go."

"Not so fast!" Danny reached over and snatched the camera from Sotere. He pointed it at Sotere and snapped a picture. "*Now* we can go," he said. That much-needed humor helped mask their fear — a little.

Sotere started rummaging through his backpack again. "I thought we were going?" asked Danny, as Sotere found what he was looking for deep in the trenches of the backpack. It was a small tube. He held it in his hand and stared intently at it.

"Remember in ITR training; they said to put this crap all over us to blend in with our surroundings?" Sotere squeezed some camouflage paint out of the tube and began caking it on his face.

"Yeah, I remember," said Danny. "But that looks funny, man. You sure you're supposed to use that much?"

"Yeah! They said to put it mainly on the cheekbones and anything else that shines."

"Alright then — give me some of that crap," commanded Danny. "I guess we'd better do the tree limb deal too, huh?"

After they had put on their war paint like an Indian brave preparing for battle, they broke small limbs and twigs and stuck them in their helmet band. They looked at each other and struggled to stay silent as they cracked up at their reindeer-like appearance. They then nodded at each other and began to creep out of their hiding place.

Sporadic gunfire could be heard in the near distance. These two brothers-in-arms began to meticulously make their way through the jungle in search of their unit; or any friendly troops, for that matter. Low-crawling and inching through the vegetation foot by foot, Danny and Sotere finally saw a lonely yellow flare soaring through the sky in the distance. A yellow flare signified friendly troops. A sense of relief came over the boys, but they weren't there yet. After what seemed like five days — but was in reality only a few more minutes — they reached the American lines.

The Marines within the American lines saw the movement, and began to position a resistance to take out the hostiles when they realized that Danny and Sotere were friendlies. Miracle upon miracles, Danny and Sotere had found their own unit. When they got close enough, a grizzled Marine veteran looked at them and asked, "Where the h*ll have you boots been?"

"Sir, we got separated from everyone coming off the copter at the LZ," said Danny.

"Well, sh*t happens sometimes," stated the veteran. "Especially during a hot LZ. Glad you made it back. You two need to go in and report to the commanding officer and let him know who you are."

Danny and Sotere carried their backpacks and rifles to the center of the makeshift command area. As they entered, they asked the first Marine they saw to point them to the commanding officer (CO). Before long, they were directed to a stern-looking man who had a chin chiseled enough to have been forged in the fires of Hades. His name was Lieutenant Colonel Harry E. Atkinson, and he was now approaching the two young men.

As the Colonel approached, Sotere noticed that he wore no insignia on his bland green uniform. High-ranking officers in the bush didn't want to become a prime target for enemy snipers, so the tradition was born of wearing no insignia to mask their rank.

The Colonel wasn't in the best of moods. Of course, he had just lost several men in the fiery helicopter crash a few hours ago, but Danny got the impression that this mood was an everlasting constant.

Danny and Sotere snapped to attention and saluted with the crispness and form of boot camp graduation. Colonel Atkinson stopped about thirty inches in front of them and began to glare at the boys. The Colonel's jaw clenched as his eyes stalked over their boots and uniforms, stopping at the tree limbs hanging out of their helmets. He glanced at a lieutenant to his left who was chewing out another boot. The Colonel then turned back to Danny and Sotere. They had the feeling they were about to receive the same treatment.

The Colonel glanced back, shook his head, and chuckled. With a twinkle in his eyes and a cheerfulness the boys didn't think existed in him, the Colonel asked, "What do we have here? A couple of walking trees?"

"Sir, yes Sir!" screamed Danny and Sotere in unison.

"Where the h*ll have you ladies been?" shouted the Colonel with equal intensity.

Sotere tried to explain, but the Colonel couldn't understand his accent and broken English, which tended to get worse whenever he was nervous.

"Where the h*ll you from, boy?" demanded the Colonel.

"Cleveland, Sir!"

"You ain't from no sh*tting Cleveland boy! Where are you really from?" screamed the Colonel.

"Originally Greece, Sir!"

"Greece? Crap! Boy, there's only two kinds of ladies that come from Greece — Queers and Steers." The Colonel took a step closer toward Sotere. Their faces were now mere inches apart. The Colonel glared into Sotere's brown eyes and loudly asked, "Boy, which one are you?"

"Steer, Sir!"

"You had better be! How the h*ll did you get in my Marine Corps?"

"I volunteered, Sir," stated Sotere. "I am now an American Citizen."

"Well, aren't you special?" The Colonel paused and then continued, "Ladies, let me tell you what I am going to do." He chuckled as he pointed to a destination a number of yards away. "I am going to let you dig me a crapper over there. How's that grab your a**es, ladies?"

"Sir, yes Sir. Looking forward to it, Sir!" yelled the boys.

"Now, go dig my crapper and then go and report to your Squad Leader and let him know you are alive," said the Colonel. "Now get out of here and out of my face!"

"Sir, yes Sir!"

So much for friends in high places. If they could survive being a "boot," they might just make it through this thing. Danny and Sotere took out a small entrenching tool and started to dig the crapper so the Colonel could do his business. It was slow going, as they had to dig through the dense jungle vegetation.

As they were digging, Sotere leaned in close to Danny and whispered, "I always heard that sh*t flowed downhill. Now I know what that means." Danny laughed. Sotere always knew how to find the humor in the crappiest of situations.

As Danny dug, he reminisced, recalling previous times Sotere kept his head up in harsh circumstances. "Hey, remember the time in boot camp when Gunny Plummer made you crawl around and 'bah' like a sheep?" laughed Danny.

"Yeah. Don't remind me," said Sotere.

At boot camp, the Drill Instructor's job is to prepare the lowly boot to survive during combat. That meant discipline. Lots of discipline. On said day, Sotere had made the grave error of answering the Gunny Sergeant with the phrase "You said," instead of addressing him with the appropriate "The Drill Instructor said." Now, what is the big deal, you ask? Well, a "Ewe" is a female sheep, and the drill instructors didn't want to be called anything that sounded like a female sheep.

So, for his punishment — and discipline training — Gunny Plummer forced Sotere to crawl on all fours outside the barracks, "bah"ing like a sheep as the rest of the Marines watched. All the while, Gunny Plummer followed close behind Sotere, yelling, "WHAT IS A FEMALE SHEEP CALLED, YOU MAGGOT?"

"An ewe, Sir!" screamed back Sotere.

"I TOLD YOU NOT TO CALL ME A FEMALE SHEEP, YOU MAGGOT! DO YOU UNDERSTAND ME?"

"Sir, yes Sir, Drill Instructor Sir!"

It was a hard lesson, but one that was well learned. Discipline could save your life. Sloppy actions kill you — and fellow Marines!

Well, back to the digging. It had been about an hour, and Danny and Sotere were making good progress on the Colonel's real estate when he came back to check on his new makeshift toilet. He seemed pleased. He gave a little nod and said, "Well, I didn't know you had it in you. That is one first-class crapper. Good job! Now go report to your squad leader and get your assignments for tonight."

They finally found their squad leader, Corporal Kessler. Kessler took one look at them and just shook his head and smiled. "What happened to your guys?"

"Sir, we got separated from everyone coming off the chopper," said Danny.

"Remember, don't 'Sir' me out here. That can get me killed. I am just Corporal Kessler. I am glad you guys are ok."

"Yes, Corporal," said Danny.

"A hot LZ can be some scary sh*t! When that happens, as you found out, it is every man for himself until we can regroup. You did the right thing, and you made it back here alive. That is saying something. Now go get that crap off your face and those trees out of your helmets. Then get some shut-eye and some grub. You guys have a big night ahead of you. You're going on an ambush." The day just kept getting better for Danny and Sotere.

Corporal Kessler led three different four-man Fire Teams. In all, they made up the First Squad. A Fire Team is very maneuverable because of its small numbers, but at the same time carries a great deal of firepower. Kessler was a true leader. Even though he was just a few years older than Danny and Sotere, he seemed like a wise old man, and they trusted him implicitly. They had only met him the day before, but they had a good feeling about him and felt like they had known him for years.

For this dangerous duty, Danny and Sotere were teamed up with Nick, a skinny, Italian street kid from Philly, and Wells, a rugged country kid from Arkansas. They were veterans; they had been in 'Nam a whole three days. They were now known as First Squad Fire Team #1.

The ambush mission was to have the Fire Team hike out about 100 yards from the camp and become the early warning alarm if the enemy was spotted approaching the American lines. The dangerous part of the mission was that the soldiers were alone without immediate support from the rest of the company. They might have to engage the enemy and hold the line until the reinforcements could come to help. The battlefield was in the enemy's backyard, so they were incredibly skilled at watching and knowing where the Americans were at all times. On the other hand, the Americans hardly ever knew where the Viet Cong and North Vietnamese Army were hiding. The boys were ordered to stay there all night — that is, unless they were engaged by the enemy before morning.

As darkness fell upon Southeast Asia, the four boots started on their journey. They trudged into the dark, dreary jungle. The monsoon weather had hit hard that night. The rain was relentless and bitterly cold. Imagine darkness so thick that you can't even see your hand in front of your face, let alone the enemy. As they reached their destination in the dense jungle, the four boots dug a makeshift foxhole. It wasn't very deep, partially because they were exhausted from the day's adventure. Danny thought his *second day* in Vietnam would last forever.

About 20 yards from their position was a three-man Listening Post that had a night vision camera. Part of Fire Team #1's job was to protect this Listening Post. On ambushes, one man is always on watch while the others try to sleep. But in reality, how can you sleep when the NVA and Viet Cong are breathing down your neck?

Danny took the first watch. As he sat there in the pitch black, straining his eyes to see an enemy who was unseen and listening for one that was unheard, his thoughts wandered back to a time and place that seemed like a lifetime ago. He thought about the Marines who had died in the fiery helicopter crash. He felt sadness for their families and guilt for his thankfulness that he wasn't one of those Marines.

He thought about the drill instructors during training who would walk through the barracks in the middle of the night. With Marines lying in bed on either side of them as they walked down the center aisle, they would say in a loud voice: "Look around, ladies. Many of you here won't be alive in six months. Many of you are going to die. God made Marines to die." Danny could still hear in his thoughts the Marines who cried and whimpered at night.

Danny thought about his decision to become a Marine — and the one he almost made that would have sent him down a totally different path. Danny had been on his own since he was fourteen years old. It was a tough childhood. The months leading up to Danny becoming a Marine were very tough. He had lost his job parking cars, and he even had lost his old 57 Chevy in a pool game. He had no money, was being evicted from his one-room apartment, and had received a draft notice to report to the Army in a few weeks.

This is where the two pivotal decisions of Danny's young life intersected. He made a habit of frequently visiting a local watering hole. There he would attempt to drown his thoughts and emotions in his favorite brew. Quite often, he would drink with the local Marine recruiter. Danny loved how majestic the man's dress blue uniform looked. He looked almost like royalty, but in a tough, heroic sort of way. The Marine recruiter attempted to sell Danny on joining the Marines several times. As of yet, Danny wasn't buying.

There was an old man who used to drink at the bar. He was rich beyond words, or so he wanted people to think. Quite often, the old man would flip out his wallet and buy a round for the entire bar.

One night, Danny's circumstances had turned his thoughts a storm gray. He thought to himself as he hustled pool, "I'll rob that old man, take his money, and life will be easier." It's funny how stormy thoughts will appear to be bright and sunny when they first enter our minds. Danny started to form a plan.

Danny walked up to the old man and asked if he could speak to him outside. As the man followed Danny out the old, weathered bar door, he asked Danny, "Son, what do you want?"

Danny looked at him, poised to do what he thought he must do. In a split second, his heart melted, and he knew he couldn't go through with it. He wasn't raised that way. That was not who he was. He looked up at the old man with moisture forming in his eyes and said, "I just wanted to thank you for being so nice to me, and for buying me some beers."

The old man put his hand behind Danny's head almost as though cradling a young child, looked at the distraught young man, and said, "You are welcome, son. That was nice of you to say."

That one decision saved Danny's future and sent it in a totally opposite direction. He felt a sensation of relief about not robbing the old man. At the same time, he felt great anxiety for the future. What would he do? Where would he go? How would he take care of himself?

Pondering those thoughts in his drunken state, Danny stumbled down the road toward his one-room apartment. Upon reaching the door, he discovered he couldn't get in. Had they evicted him from the building already? He then heard a police officer yell, "Freeze, kid!"

Surprised and puzzled, Danny tried to turn the doorknob again. It was then that he realized that this was not his apartment building at all. This was a business. The cop thought he was breaking into a business. "Uh oh! I am in trouble," he thought to himself. Out of instinct more than anything else, Danny took off running down the sidewalk. The police officer was in hot pursuit. The officer's partner joined the chase, and the two gained on the troubled teen.

Danny finally found the right door and hurriedly turned the knob. He flew up the three flights of stairs like a gazelle on a flat prairie and flung open the unlocked door to his room. He always kept his room unlocked, for there was nothing to steal. He quickly dove under his bed and waited.

The cops were now on his floor. Danny heard them talking, but couldn't quite make out their words. It sounded like they were opening every apartment door. He then heard the creak of his door as it swung open. Straining his eyes, Danny saw the well-worn shoes of the two beat cops. "Where the h*ll did that kid go?" asked one of the cops.

"I don't know," said his partner. "He ran like a jackrabbit. Let's get out of here. He didn't steal anything." With that, Danny heard the thump of his door being shut and the footsteps becoming a distant sound down the hallway.

Danny exhaled deeply. For the first time, he realized he had held his breath all the while the police officers were in his room. At that moment, he decided to take charge of his life; if it wasn't too late. The next morning, Danny decided not to wait for his draft notice with the Army. And on that very day, Danny became a United States Marine.

With that, Danny's thoughts suddenly shook him back to the present, to a foxhole in Southeast Asia with an inwardness and personification that frightened him. *Would he die tonight? How would he handle it when the firefight began? Would he fight or would he become paralyzed with fear?* Danny didn't like those thoughts, but unfortunately, he couldn't explore them anymore that night. He took some comfort in the fact that Gunnery Sergeant Plummer believed in him. On the day Danny graduated from boot camp, Gunnery Sergeant Plummer had pulled him aside, rested a hand on his shoulder, and said, "Lane, you're going to make it." Danny didn't know what Gunner Plummer saw in him, but he sure hoped he was right.

Suddenly, the silence of his thoughts was abruptly interrupted with the squeal of a loudspeaker. A man's voice shattered the silence with thick, broken English: "Joe, we have one of your soldiers. GI Joe . . . Bob Burrows, Serial Number 2461167. He is alive and if you want to live, give yourself up too. Come over to our side, Joe! We will send you home, and not kill you like the other Joes." That ear-piercing voice sent a shiver through the night. The voice repeated its message over and over again like a bad horror movie. The rest of the fire team crawled towards the foxhole and prepared for the inevitable.

Then there was a loud POP. That brought the four boys to full alert. What was that? It sounded like a cork being pulled out of a champagne bottle. A devastating chill shook Danny's spirit as his realization came into focus. That POP was the sound a Chinese Communist grenade made when it was activated. They then heard a faint, small thud a few feet behind their foxhole. Danny instinctively yelled, "Incoming!"

The grenade exploded and rocked the four young men. Danny could feel dirt and debris rained down on his body. He lifted his head a couple of inches and looked over at Sotere. The Greek was fine, too. Danny saw in the shadows that Nick and Wells appeared to be fine as well. Danny thought a small prayer of thanks.

Their good fortune immediately ended as "Charlie[1]" opened up on them with automatic weapons. Their little foxhole was being bombarded by bullets. Debris and dirt covered the four boots. How they managed not to get hit was a miracle upon miracles.

Technically, they weren't boots anymore, but that didn't comfort them. They were virgins in the world of combat. The four "grunts" nervously hesitated, hunkering down in their foxhole. Time seemed to slow down, but it was actually only a few seconds. Somebody had to do something, but it was so hard. Fear had paralyzed the four grunts. And can we blame them? What would we do if we shared that foxhole with them on that fateful night?

Danny's mind raced to Gunner Plummer. What would he say at this moment? "Lane, man up! Just like in training! Do your job!" A small dose of courage welled up inside of Danny. He raised his shoulder just a bit and threw an illumination grenade to light up the area around their hole. With any luck, they would be able to at least see the silhouettes of Charlie. Danny then activated the switch that controlled the claymore mine they had positioned in front of their foxhole. Steel balls flew from the mine in multiple directions. Would it be enough to protect them?

Sotere, Nick, and Wells popped the pins on their M-26 grenades and launched them towards the incoming gunfire. The main company then threw illumination grenades. The night sky was now lit up like a Christmas tree. Danny's knees seemed to buckle with fear. He knew they needed to fire back, or death

---

[1] The enemy in Vietnam was known as the Viet Cong. This was shortened to VC. In the NATO designation that was known as "Victor Charlie" which the troops simply shortened to "Charlie."

would be their destination, but his body wasn't obeying his thoughts. Ever so slightly, he scooted himself closer to the foxhole rim. He raised his eyes over the rim and saw the shadowy figures of Charlie headed their way.

"Here they come! Get ready! Let's do this!" Danny screamed. Courage and reality overcame fear, and the grunts unleashed their M-16 machine guns on the enemy. They emptied 30-round clips one after another as fast as they could. The enemy retaliated with equal fury.

Before long, they heard a scream in the background. With sweat pouring down their bodies despite the cold, wet rain, the four grunts heard the scream again. The scream seemed to pierce the chaos all around them.

Sotere yelled, "It is one of our Listening Post soldiers. I am going to get him. Cover me!" As Sotere scrambled toward the wounded Marine, Danny, Nick, and Wells laid down cover fire. Sotere picked up the Marine, threw him over his shoulder, and headed toward the command center and the main company.

Danny, Nick, and Wells continued to lay down cover fire. All of a sudden — there was nothing. An eerie, quiet calm surrounded the entire battlefield. Nick looked at Wells and then at Danny. They all were puzzled. What had happened? Had the NVA and Viet Cong left? Or were they all dead? Maybe the enemy troops were playing possum and were poised to blow the boys' heads off if they appeared out of their foxhole.

Nonetheless, it was time to move. Danny, Nick, and Wells slowly crept out of their hole, which had served them so well, and headed back towards the security of the company lines. Finally, they made it to the main unit like three pups finding their way home to nestle into their mother's protection.

All members of Fire Team #1 had faced their first firefight and survived. Corporal Kessler greeted them with a smile and a slap on the shoulder. After being reunited with Sotere, the world felt a little bit more complete — as complete as it could in a jungle in Southeast Asia.

Colonel Atkinson walked up to the four Marines and said, "Well done Marines. I am going to put all of you in for a medal for bravery under fire. Again, well done."

That night, Danny, Sotere, Nick, and Wells all understood what was meant by the Marine Corp creed: "My Rifle." They had heard the words many times before, but they had been just words. Now, the words meant more.

MY RIFLE

This is my rifle. There are many like it, but this one is mine.

My rifle is my best friend. It is my life. I must master it as I must master my life.

My rifle, without me, is useless. Without my rifle, I am useless. I must fire my rifle true. I must shoot straighter than my enemy who is trying to kill me. I must shoot him before he shoots me. I will . . .

My rifle and I know that what counts in war is not the rounds we fire, the noise of our burst, nor the smoke we make. We know that it is the hits that count. We will hit . . .

My rifle is human, even as I, because it is my life. Thus, I will learn it as a brother. I will learn its weaknesses, its strength, its parts, its accessories, its sights and its barrel. I will keep my rifle clean and ready, even as I am clean and ready. We will become part of each other. We will . . .

Before God, I swear this creed. My rifle and I are the defenders of my country. We are the masters of our enemy. We are the saviors of my life.

So be it, until victory is America's and there is no enemy, but peace!

When morning came, Danny, Sotere, Nick, and Wells joined the other Marines in patrolling the area where the engagement had happened during the night. They were looking for any signs of the dead enemy soldiers or any intelligence that might prove useful. What they found was surprising and disturbing.

"Where are all the dead bodies?" asked Sotere.

"I don't know," replied Danny.

"Hey, guys! Look over here," said Nick. "Look at these: blood trails, but no bodies."

"I have heard of this type of thing by the Cong," said Wells. "I guess it is their version of leave no man behind. They drag their dead out after the battle. I heard it also has to do with them not wanting us to know how many of theirs we whacked."

The main objective of Operation Meade River was to search out and destroy the enemy. Danny and the five thousand other Marines involved in the operation occupied a piece of land not much larger than your neighborhood. All those Marines and all that equipment were focused on just a three by five square mile track from the center of Dodge City. For the next ten days, the Marines methodically and strategically closed the noose a little tighter around the Viet Cong and North Vietnamese Army.

The Marines' job was to root out the enemy within the closing noose. Charlie was a master of concealment. You could walk right by them and not know it until they cut you down or slit your throat.

In order to combat this sly, treacherous enemy, the Marines would walk in a line, about fifteen yards apart. They were looking for spider holes and underground bunkers which hid the enemy. At night, the Marines would form a perimeter and dig foxholes about twenty yards apart, with four men in each foxhole. They would pitch tents which were made out of their waterproof ponchos. If they could get an empty ammo box, they would sleep on them so that their weary body could get off of the monsoon-soaked ground.

The only food was C-Rations, which consisted of one small, flat can, one large can, and two other, smaller cans. Each C-Ration had a meat-based item, a bread item, and a dessert item. After a while, the taste didn't bother you so much, and you even looked forward to dinner time. This was gourmet out in the bush.

The sweep and destroy mission included the rice paddies and surrounding area that covered most of the lowlands. Rice paddies were everywhere, and the Cong loved to conceal themselves underneath the water. They would breathe through a bamboo straw and wait for an unsuspecting American, then emerge from the watery swamp and attack their victim. Afterwards, they disappeared again into the depths of the swamp.

The Marines had to walk on the strip of land between rice paddies called a dike. The dikes were very muddy, slippery, and narrow. Each step that was taken was done with elaborate care. Not only because of the slip hazard, but more importantly because of the booby trap hazard. You never knew if your next step would be your last.

The hardest fighting of the operation commenced on December 1st as the 3/5 Marines encountered a large enemy bunker complex along its right flank. This became known as the *Hook*. All of a sudden, the Marines began to receive heavy fire from a tree line about a hundred yards away. Danny and his Fire Team hit the ground. The other Fire Teams followed suit. Some of the Marines made it to the ground of their own volition. Some, in the other Fire Teams, weren't so lucky. They were cut down in the prime of life by the firestorm of bullets. Bullets flew over Danny's head and hit the ground a few feet from him.

"Return Fire!" yelled Corporal Kessler. "Repeat! Return Fire! Corpsman up!"

The entire Company returned fire into the unseen enemy, somewhere in the dense clump of trees. Danny and his comrades continued to fire, but heavier fire came back in their direction. They were pinned down. What should they do now? If they moved, they were dead. If they attacked, they were dead. Marines dropping were as thick as the tree line.

"We have to get to those Marines. Lay down cover fire and rescue those Marines," came the order from the Commanding Officer. Danny, Sotere, Nick, and Wells did as they were told. They stood up, put their fear aside, and did their job. They laid down heavy fire and ran to their comrades. Danny grabbed a body and began to haul him out of the line of fire. He didn't know whether the Marine was alive or dead. He and his fellow Marines hauled the wounded and dead back to a secure area where the corpsman could help them — if he could.

The radio observer wiped the grime and dirt off the knobs on his radio. He activated it and called, "FDC. Headquarters! This is Bravo/Tango/Alpha ... Mike 3/5 ... We need medivac helicopters, and we need them now. Marines are down. Grid 734596, Direction 4800. LZ is secure!"

After a brief buzz of static, a voice came from the speaker on the heavy-duty portable radio. "Roger, BTA — medivac is on its way."

The radio observer relaxed for a moment and sighed. The problem was that the helicopters had to come from Danang, which was at least thirty minutes away. Many of the Marines would be gone by then. But maybe a few of the wounded could be saved.

The enemy assault continued to rain down on the Marines. They couldn't dig in low enough in the soft Vietnamese terrain. At that moment, some help arrived. Bell UH-1 Iroquois Helicopters, known by the troops as "Huey Gunships," came low over the horizon. These helicopters were a welcome sight. They had a lot of firepower for helicopters. Their armaments included two M60 machine guns and two rocket pods. But then Danny heard it — and saw it a moment later. The enormous shadow of "Puff the Magic Dragon" flew over the horizon. "Puff" was the unofficial name for the large, four-prop engine plane developed by McDonnell Douglas and given the designation AC-47 Spooky.

"Puff" soared over the horizon and began peppering the tree line with guns and rockets. It carried a six-barrel, Gatling-style gun with rotating barrels that was reminiscent of the old West, but with much more firepower. These guns could fire up to 6,000 rounds per minute. Danny and his fellow Marines needed every bit of that firepower.

The tree line erupted into light and flame. It looked like the night sky over Manhattan on the Fourth of July. Under the cover of the assault, Danny and his fellow Marines were able to scamper out and retrieve more wounded and dead.

Danny laid the body he was carrying onto the soft turf and leaned over his comrade to get a better look at his condition. He was unresponsive. At that moment, the corpsman knelt down beside Danny and began checking out the fallen Marine. After a moment, the corpsman looked at Danny and just shook his head from side to side. The corpsman got up into a crouch and hurried off to check on the next wounded Marine.

Many Marines died that day, and dozens were wounded. The Company commander pulled the Marines back and had them dig in for the night. Tomorrow would be another day to fight.

The next morning, December 2, 1968, was a terrible morning. Think back on your childhood when you came down with the flu. Remember that feeling? On that morning in Southeast Asia, it was very much like that, minus the flu. Instead of the flu, the Marines were greeted with a tremendous monsoon rain that was so cold it rattled their bones. The lowlands were already flooded, and made ground movements forward almost impossible.

Even so, the Marines moved forward and attacked the enemy "Hook" fortress again and again. Each assault had the same result: disaster. Each step forward was greeted with a peppering of bullets from the tree line. Finally, the CO had had enough and decided to wait for better weather and conditions to advance on the enemy.

The next morning, December 3, 1968, didn't look much better. The rain was still coming down as if there were profit in it, and the thin blades of elephant grass were doing a lousy job of protecting the Marines from the onslaught from the enemy. Danny hunkered back down into the muddy soil in an attempt to get as low as possible. It was now obvious that the enemy was heavily fortified, and on this day, they were barking for a fight.

The 11th Marine Artillery spent most of the previous day and night conducting coordinated missions to rage destructive force into the Hook, but the 3/5 continued taking on casualties from the entrenched enemy firepower. Troops from the 3/26 were then moved from their screening positions in order to help the 3/5 in the attack.

In terms of overall position, the enemy was trapped. They were heavily fortified in their "hook" fortress, but they were completely surrounded. There was no escape. The Viet Cong and NVA had two options: surrender or fight. And they had chosen the latter.

On the morning of December 4, 1968, the CO asked for air strikes. No, he demanded them. If the enemy wanted to stay and fight, then they were going to learn what fighting was all about. Throughout the day, the reinforced Marines successfully moved closer to the tree line. After repeated airstrikes dropped multiple 750-pound bombs, the Marines of the 3/26 were able to fight their way into the southernmost position of the Hook.

By nightfall, both Battalions were in place, but still had to call in additional air and artillery strikes to soften up the enemy. This time, the strikes were perilously close to the Americans' own positions. The enemy was trapped — and they knew it. The Marines were now in position for their final assault on the Hook which would commence at daybreak the next morning.

In the pre-dawn, damp air on December 5, the Commanding Officer motioned for the Vietnamese interpreter to come over to him. The interpreter half-ran and half-squatted as he hurriedly made his way through the bush to the CO. When the soldier knelt down beside him, the CO said, "Take that bullhorn and warn those ba**ards that they had better surrender, or we are going to obliterate them."

One might wonder why the Marines would warn the enemy of their coming death, and give them a chance to be relieved of this fate. Well, quite simply, because the Marines were Americans. They refused to fight like the Nazis of yesteryear or the terrorists of today. Killing and war were always the last resort. American Marines fought with honor and respected the value of life. The enemy deserved a chance to surrender, and they were going to give it to them.

The interpreter grabbed the bullhorn and began to speak, "Charlie, bạn được bao quanh. Bạn không có cơ hội để tồn tại các cuộc không kích. Hãy đầu hàng bây giờ và sống để xem gia đình của bạn một lần nữa. Chúng tôi sẽ coi bạn với danh dự và tôn trọng. Bạn có chỉ là một vài phút trước khi thenapalm giảm xuống có nghĩa là cái chết chắc chắn của bạn. Đi ra bây giờ với hai bàn tay của bạn cao và bạn sẽ không bị tổn hại."

The translation was: "Charlie, you are surrounded. You have no chance to survive the air strikes. Please surrender NOW and live to see your family again. We will treat you with honor and respect. You have just a few minutes before napalm is dropped, meaning your sure death. Come out now, with your hands high, and you will not be harmed."

The interpreter had barely lowered the bullhorn when massive gunfire began to rain down on the Marines again.

When the storm was silent, the CO rose up on his elbows and yelled at the interpreter: "Tell them again!"

The interpreter repeated the message, and immediately the Marines again received the enemy's hostile response.

"Light the fools up!" yelled the CO.

Within several minutes, two Marine Phantom F-4 fighter jets soared overhead. The roar of their engines was a welcome sound to the pinned-down Marines. The vibrations from their powerful engines shook the ground, and hopefully, fear into the enemy.

The F-4s swooped down and dropped napalm on the tree line and on the heads of the hidden Viet Cong and North Vietnamese Army. They then swung around and made another run. This time, they dropped 500-pound bombs on the tree line. Danny had never experienced anything like this before. To hear about it was one thing — to witness it was completely different.

Napalm is extremely flammable, and sticks to practically everything. It is an awful way to die. It burns one alive. That is why the enemy was given the chance to surrender. It was the right thing to do — the American thing to do. When the 500-pounders exploded, it was as if the Gates of Hades had erupted upon the tree line. Hot flames enveloped in black smoke shot straight up and out in all directions. Could anyone have survived that?

Believe it or not, when the Marines started to move forward again they still received some enemy fire from the tree line. It was spread out, and not nearly as much as before, but was still deadly.

After the inferno dissipated, the CO gave his men the dreaded command.

"Listen up, Marines," yelled the commander. "We are going to have to do this the hard way. The MARINE WAY! On foot! Go in there and take those suckers out!"

Danny and his fellow Marines crept ever so cautiously towards the burning inferno, which at one time was the tree line. They engaged the enemy one fortified bunker at a time. The enemy still had a lot of fight in them. Some had to be physically taken out hand to hand. No training simulation could have prepared Danny and the Marines for this type of warfare. It was brutal. It was uncivilized. It was kill or be killed. Survival was the ultimate objective. Using explosives and flame throwers to terminate and capture the last of the VC and NVA, the Marines, at last, had the tree line secure.

The Marines began to look around to see what was so important to the enemy that they would fight so hard to keep this location in their hands. They discovered a heavily-fortified underground command center for the Viet Cong Doc Lap Battalion.

Carnage was everywhere. Burned enemy soldiers were almost unrecognizable as human. The smell was even worse. Holding his hand over his mouth and nose to filter what he could of the air, Danny said, "Man, I have never seen anything like this before. Those films back in training sure didn't prepare us for this."

"You ain't kiddin," said Wells. "They look like crispy critters. It is almost unbelievable."

"Why wouldn't they just give up?" asked Nick.

"I don't know," said Danny. "You would think being a POW would be more inviting to them then burning alive."

"Well, for one thing," chimed in the Greek, "that underground bunker back there. Also, these guys were hardcore. True warriors. They would have probably been dishonored if they surrendered. Burning to death probably looked better under the circumstances."

"Collect as much info as you can from this place. Keep looking around, Marines," said the CO. After they gathered as much information as was useful, he said, "Alright. Blow it up." They took explosives and destroyed the underground command center, so no one would ever be able to use it again.

When the smoke cleared, they discovered more than 100 dead enemy soldiers, and captured another fifteen. Transport helicopters were called in to take the enemy POWs to the Marine Division Headquarters in Da Nang. There they would be processed and interrogated to gather more intel.

Navy Seabees flew in with their massive equipment and bulldozed a mass grave for the dead enemy soldiers. The Seabees have been instrumental in every American war for the last 75 years. Their motto of "We build, we fight" pretty much says it all. Over those many years, the Seabees have been the most elite construction crews the world has ever seen.

After the Seabees had finished their gruesome duty, the CO ordered Fire Team #1 and the entire Company to move out. The enemy was a wounded animal, and the noose had to be tightened.

The Company trekked through the jungle for another click or so, and then began looking for a place to set up a perimeter for the night. Danny, Sotere, Nick, and Wells began looking for a place to set up their own little fort for the night in a densely-covered area within the perimeter.

As he was searching for a safe place, Danny came across what appeared to be a freshly-dug grave under some jungle vegetation. He immediately reported his finding to Corporal Kessler. Kessler went and reported the finding to the CO.

The Corporal had been gone for just a few minutes when he returned and gave Danny the dreaded news. "Lane, the CO said that since you found him, you dig him up and see what you can find . . . Hey, be careful! They booby-trap them sometimes."

"What a way to get intel," Danny thought to himself. "Another boot assignment, I guess. When will they see me as a grunt and not a boot? How much action do you have to see to get some respect?"

Nick and Wells wanted nothing to do with the dead body. "Man, I am not touching it!" said Wells. "Digging up a grave is some bad karma."

"He's right, man! I ain't doing it either," said Nick.

Sotere shook his head. "I will help you, Dan Bo. I ain't afraid of no corpse."

Danny and Sotere began the macabre duty that was placed before them. As they began to dig, they uncovered a body that had been neatly wrapped in an illumination parachute. The soldier was a North Vietnamese Army regular. He had obviously been killed in the Marines' attack. Rigor mortis hadn't set in completely. In their haste to retreat, the NVA knew they couldn't take their fallen comrade with them, but they gave him an honorable burial.

Danny went through the soldier's pockets and discovered a letter and a picture of a woman and two children. He took the letter and searched for the Company Vietnamese interpreter — the same man who had used the bullhorn that morning.

When he had found him, Danny asked, "Can you read this letter for me? I found it on a dead NVA soldier."

The interpreter took the folded up piece of paper that Danny handed him. He smoothed it out a bit to make it more legible, and began to read it to himself.

"Gửi tình yêu,

Những đứa trẻ và tôi yêu và nhớ em rất nhiều. Xin được an toàn và trở lại với chúng tôi ngay. Người vợ yêu thương của bạn."

He then translated it for Danny:

"Dear Love,

The kids and I love and miss you so very much. Please be safe and return to us soon.

Your loving wife."

Danny's mouth hung open with the shock. That letter had deep meaning. The words of love and concern expressed in the letter hit Danny hard. It was as if he had taken a grenade to the gut. "It was from his wife! Those are his kids in the picture!" thought Danny. Those thoughts played over and over through his head like a vinyl going around a phonograph.

That soldier was just like him. He was just a guy fighting for his beliefs and his country. He had a family. He had kids. That was the first time that Danny saw the enemy as people, and not as some sort of monster.

Still holding the picture in his hand, Danny walked up to his fellow Fire Team #1 comrades. "Look at this picture. I found it in that dude's pocket. He had a wife and kids and everything."

Danny handed the tattered photo to Nick. Nick glanced at it but said nothing. Looking over Nick's shoulder at the picture, Wells said, "So what, man? He would have slit our throats if he had been given the chance."

"All I am saying is that he was a lot like us. You know, we are all people, stuck in this crap hole . . . Anyway, you guys go dig in. I am going to sleep here. My bed is already made, and I am tired."

"Here?" asked Nick. "Man, that is creepy, dude." Pointing to the dead man's grave, Nick continued, "You really going to sleep in that hole?"

"Suit yourself," said Wells.

Danny respectfully laid the corpse in some nearby brush and then climbed into the grave. He lay there for a few minutes, but he couldn't rest. Out of respect for the dead soldier and the family he left behind, Danny laid him back in his final resting place and placed the picture of his family over his heart. Danny then said a little prayer and covered him with dirt. He felt a devastating anguish in his gut for the man's family. Those kids would never receive another hug from their daddy. That wife would never receive another gentle kiss from her loving husband. War is inevitable in the course of history. War is even needed at times, but war is always such a waste.

On December 6, 1968, the 3/5 Marines parted company with the 3/26 Marines and turned Northward and commenced a sweep of Dodge City from West to East. Danny's Regiment, the 3/5, was then pulled off the operation to fulfill other priorities.

Unbelievably, killing was now becoming routine. Danny, Sotere, Combat, and Wells grew up a great deal in the short nineteen days it took for the entire operation. They not only learned how to survive, and how combat is fought and won, but also about themselves. They learned that they could respond effectively during stressful situations. Fear couldn't control them. And fear would never paralyze them from taking necessary action. Danny learned how to face death in the eye daily, while still trusting God to hold him in His arms, no matter the circumstance or the results.

Operation Meade River concluded on December 9, 1968. *Stars & Stripes* Newspaper reported that 108 Marines lost their lives in the operation. Another 513 were wounded. *Stars & Stripes* also reported that there were 1,325 confirmed enemy casualties.

It was estimated that another 3,000 enemy soldiers' bodies would never be found, because they were obliterated by the pinpoint accuracy of the American bombings from heavy artillery, fixed-wing aircraft like the F-4 Phantom, and battleships such as the most decorated battleship in US history, the *New Jersey*. The *New Jersey*, also known as "Big J" or "Black Dragon," had an armament which included nine of the devastating, 16 inch, .50 caliber Mark 7 guns, which could hit a bullseye at a distance upward of 58 miles.

Even though it seemed like an eternity for those who had to live through it, Danny and the Marines of Fire Team #1 realized that nineteen days was just a speck of time. And in that speck, 108 American families lost their loved ones to the reality of war, and would feel the pains from that scar the rest of their lives.

A COUPLE of hours after the ambulance brought him in, Danny was lying in a bed in a private room in the Intensive Care Unit of St. Mary's Hospital in Huntington, WV. It was now 2006. Dr. McComas stood beside Danny's bed with a chart in his hand. He gently touched Danny's left leg in the hopes of awakening him. Danny slowly opened his eyes and strained to focus on the shadowy figure standing at his bedside.

"Mr. Lane, I am Dr. McComas. I am a neurosurgeon. Do you know where you are?"

Danny showed no responsiveness whatsoever. Dr. McComas continued, "Mr. Lane, you are in the Intensive Care Unit at St. Mary's hospital." Pointing to Chris, the doctor continued, "This is your son, Chris. He was here last night too. Do you remember anything about last night?" Danny responded with a very slight shake of his head from left to right.

"Can you remember my name?" asked Dr. McComas. The doctor paused for a few seconds and then said, "I just told you a couple of minutes ago. Do you remember?"

Danny's face wrinkled with the strain of putting together a thought. He opened his mouth, but nothing came out. Then, slowly, he said, "Doc, Doctor . . . I dunno."

"McComas. My name is Dr. McComas, and your name is Danny Lane," said the doctor. "You are at St. Mary's Hospital, in Huntington, West Virginia. Do you know what year it is?

Danny thought for a long moment, then hesitantly said in thick, slurred speech, "I don't know, 1969?"

"It's 2006, Mr. Lane. I want you to try to remember that. I am attempting to determine whether you have short-term memory loss. So, each time we talk, I am going to ask you some specific questions, to see what you can recall. Do you know your name now?" No response. Danny's blank stare and empty eyes concerned Dr. McComas. With great sympathy, the doctor said, "Your name is Danny . . . Danny Lane."

"I discovered from your son, Chris, that you are a veteran, and saw a lot of action during the Vietnam War," continued Dr. McComas. "He also mentioned that you have been very sick for the last few months; that you vomit three or four times each day and experience night sweats and chills. Chris is also concerned that you may be experiencing flashbacks from the war because sometimes your conversations aren't making much sense. Do you remember anything about any of this?"

Again, no response from Danny. Turning to Chris, Dr. McComas said, "I have notified the VA that he is here and I have requested for them to send us his medical records. I have also ordered a CT and MRI scan of your father's head and brain. The orderlies will come and get him soon to take him for the test."

"Thank you, doctor," said a concerned Chris.

Dr. McComas gave a weak smile to Chris and then turned back to Danny. "Danny, do you remember my name now?"

Danny stared at the doctor and said uncertainly, ". . . Doctor . . . ?"

Dr. McComas smiled gently at Danny and placed his hand affectionately on his leg. "That's a start, Mr. Lane."

CHAPTER TWO

AN HOA: NOT QUITE LIKE HOME

CROUCHED IN THE VIETNAM JUNGLE, THE Marines heard a low rumble in the distance. They couldn't quite make out what it was. Their bodies tensed as adrenaline forced them to full alertness. You can imagine the relief they felt as their eyes were able to focus more clearly on the dark objects coming over the horizon — they were extraction helicopters. The Operation Meade River mission was over! Danny's shoulders slumped as his muscles relaxed and some of the stress oozed out of his body — at least for a little while. Sotere lit up a cigarette and took a long draw. A satisfied look creased his face. He exhaled the smoke in Danny's direction.

"Man, Greek!" coughed Danny. "You know that smoke chokes the crap out of me."

"It is alright my friend. Chill. It is just a little smoke," laughed Sotere.

"Chill, my foot! My mom used to blow smoke in my face too. And for a kid who had asthma, it about killed me."

"There is a lot more that can kill you out here than a little smoke," said Sotere with a chuckle in his voice.

As the C-46 helicopters made their descent into the rain-soaked landing zone, the air created by their powerful rotor blades bombarded the Marines. Sotere threw down his cigarette and steadied his helmet.

As the helicopter which was to be Fire Team #1's ticket out of the front lines landed, the door gunner readied his M-60 machine gun towards the nearby tree line. The Marines had come to learn that Charlie was everywhere and could never be trusted. A Marine who dropped his guard too far was a dead Marine.

Corporal Kessler and his Fire Teams quickly and gladly climbed aboard the huge craft. As soon as the last Marine stepped aboard, the craft lifted off and headed out of the combat zone.

A memory of his first flight nineteen days ago came to Danny's mind, and he jerked his helmet off his head and sat on it. He survived his first operation, and he wasn't about to have the enemy bite him in the butt with a bullet.

Danny looked up and saw the relief on the faces of his fellow Marines, but there was something else in their eyes. They had that "thousand-yard stare." Danny knew he wore it too — and to a certain extent would wear it the rest of his life. The "thousand-yard stare" is a certain look that all combat soldiers get when they have experienced hell on earth. Seeing death, cheating death and causing death does something to a person that never completely goes away. Boots don't wear the "stare" yet, but grunts sure do.

"Why am I alive?" thought Danny. "So many others died. I never even knew their names." These thoughts began to haunt Danny. Of course, he was relieved that he and Sotere were not flying in the back of that helicopter in body bags, but why had they survived Operation Meade River when 108 other Marines had been snuffed out? He grieved for their families. No day would ever be the same for those families again. Were those dead Marines just in the wrong place at the wrong time? Was it God's will? Danny didn't know. He tried to put his racing mind in neutral. He couldn't deal with those thoughts today. He just had to focus on living as long as he could, one day at a time — no, one moment at a time.

The group of helicopters started their descent. Heavy rains and high winds buffeted the choppers as they sat back down in systematic order on the tarmac at An Hoa Marine Base — just like they had left nineteen days before. Danny, Sotere, Wells, Nick, and their fellow Marines exited the rear door of the craft and trudged through the monsoon weather towards the 3/5 Regimental tented area. A tent to shelter him from this awful place sounded pretty good to Danny right about now.

An Hoa was located across the Vu Gia River, in what was known to the Americans as the Arizona Territory. Back in the days before the war broke out, this little piece of land was filled with quaint villages that were home to about 25,000 Vietnamese.

The sounds of children playing and families enjoying each other were long gone. All the children and teenagers had been sent to live in the larger, safer areas of Vietnam like DaNang, while only elderly citizens remained in the area hiding in bamboo and straw huts. An Hoa was now surrounded by some very different neighbors. The 5th Marine Regiment was located southeast of the Arizona Territory, while the Viet Cong and North Vietnamese army had a base inside the territory, just spitting distance away. Danny soon discovered this short distance would be of deadly consequence.

The area's remaining villagers just wanted to be left alone. They just wanted the war to be over so they could live in peace; they didn't care one way or the other about communism or democracy. They lived in huts and harvested rice fields just like their ancestors had done for centuries. That was their life, and they just wanted to get back to it. Their plight moved many compassionate Marines to visit their villages and help them.

Can you imagine being face to face with someone who appears to be a common, poor villager only to have your face blown off as they pull out a gun and shoot you or throw a grenade in your lap? That is what the Marines dealt with throughout the Vietnam War. The villagers were at the mercy of the VC and NVA. Quite often, this treacherous, cowardly enemy would plant themselves among the villagers to trick unsuspecting Americans whose compassionate spirit was to help the locals. Many times the VC and NVA wouldn't wear uniforms, but common clothes just like the villagers.

An Hoa was supposed to be away from the front lines, but as Danny and Sotere soon learned, there were no rear areas in Vietnam. An Hoa was nicknamed Rocket City because the enemy bombarded the Marines on an almost daily basis with 122mm rockets. This rocket was fin-stabilized and had the longest range of any rocket fired at the Marines: three to eleven kilometers. It was lethal within a 163 square meter burst area — think about that! A single rocket could destroy everything in a third of a mile area. That is the fear Danny lived with when he wasn't in the jungle being stalked by the enemy every minute of every day.

How do you relax in an environment like that? Everyone has to have downtime to let stress ooze away after a hard day of work and fighting the traffic. These Marines had no such luxury. They put their lives on the line 24/7 for months at a time to keep us free. Stress and weariness had to be dealt with in the midst of the most terrifying and emotionally draining experiences imaginable.

As if the rockets weren't enough, Danny and the Marines also had to deal with the "sappers." The Viet Cong Sappers were very well-trained soldiers whose duty was to find a way into the heavily fortified American compounds and wreak as much havoc and destruction as possible. They wanted to break through the maze of barbwire and defenses protecting the American lines so that their infantry could follow and attack. The sappers would crawl so quietly and slowly that if you were only a few meters from them, you would probably never know they were there.

The sappers were similar to the Japanese Suicide Kamikaze that we experienced a couple of generations ago during World War II. They would strap explosives onto their bodies and begin their evil one-way trip. Life was not precious to them; it was a tool to be used in order to gain a political end. They were going to die, and they were going to take as many American Marines with them as possible. After the sappers would consummate their deadly attack, Danny and his fellow Marines would often find heroin and cocaine on their corpses. How do you fight an enemy who is willing to get high in order to accomplish its evil ends?

The enemy also played deadly psychological games with the Marines at An Hoa. They wanted the Marines to always be off balance regarding when and where an attack would commence. By using hit and run tactics, the VC and NVA would keep the Marines from getting a good night's rest and keep them in a state of high stress.

An Hoa was also surrounded by deceptively high mountains. With practiced expertise, Charlie had learned the precise settings and coordinates on their rocket launchers to execute their deadly arsenal right into the mess hall, ammo dump, airfield, and even the tented sleeping quarters of the war-weary Marines. No place was safe at An Hoa. You couldn't even take a crap without fear of a rocket landing in your lap. Some rear area! This wasn't much safer than Danny experienced on those nineteen hellish days in the jungle.

You took your life into your own hands (or should I say into the enemy's hands) wherever you went on An Hoa Base. Fire Team #1 discovered that the hard way. On the day of their return from Operation Meade River, they strolled wearily over to the mess hall to get a well-deserved hot meal — but they got more than just a meal!

They had just gotten in the food line to wait their turn, when all of a sudden, sirens started to blare. The sirens were so loud that the four boys' bodies jerked from the shock. Immediately, their minds and bodies went on full alert. That is what nineteen days in the bush will do.

All of sudden, all the other Marines in the mess began to run for the doorway, dropping their full food trays in the process. As the trays began to hit the ground, it sounded like a continuous clanking bell accompaniment to complement the music of the blaring sirens.

Danny, Sotere, Nick, and Wells gazed at each other with inexperienced puzzlement. They then heard a woman scream at the top of her lungs. Where were all the Marines going? Why was there a woman screaming and where did she come from?

The boys quickly realized that it wasn't a woman at all. That was the sound of a 140mm rocket. There is no sound like it. Once you have heard it, it becomes branded into your consciousness forever. A Marine yelled, "Incoming!" and everyone continued their wild scramble towards the exits.

Their bodies finally answered the call of their minds' direction, and Fire Team #1 followed suit and ran outside. They dove into a heavily sandbagged bunker just as the rocket made landfall next to the bunker. If they had delayed just five more seconds, then this book would have never been written, and you wouldn't be reading it.

Several more rockets screamed overhead, and explosions riddled the compound. As he lay in the bunker flat on his belly next to Sotere, Danny lifted his head ever so slightly to see if he could view anything. He thought to himself, "Will this madness ever end?" And just like it began, suddenly it was over. Complete silence. No whine from rockets overhead. No explosions. Just bone-chilling, eerie silence.

After they were fairly confident that it was over, Danny and Sotere put their palms onto the dirt and slowly pushed themselves to their feet. With their fellow Marines, they began to slowly examine the destruction around them and look for casualties.

They could hardly believe their eyes. The mess hall was totally obliterated. Luckily, there had been no casualties. The reality of the experience hit Danny like a sock to the gut from a heavyweight

fighter. He had been in that tent when the attack commenced. He should be dead, yet he wasn't. God must have a plan for him. However, Danny promised himself never to go a mess hall tent again — a promise he kept!

Danny, Sotere, Nick, and Wells shared a large canvas tent with their twelve man squad and Corporal Kessler. This was their home away from home so to speak. This was the rear area — and for a Marine in Southeast Asia — this was as good as it got.

Now, it wasn't all work and no play. There was always a pickup basketball game going on. No breakaway rims and no glass backboards, just the usual metal tub nailed to the top of a spindly narrow pole. But it was basketball, and that was something. After a hard game, you could even take a relaxing shower standing under a 55-gallon barrel. Just don't expect the water to be too warm — but, it was wet.

The Marines' duty while in the rear area was straightforward. If they weren't on bunker watch duty, then they went on patrols. At first glance, it wasn't much different from the front lines, but getting to sleep in a tent rather than on jungle dirt made a big difference.

The Marines slept on small canvas cots within their tents. They always slept with their clothes and boots on, and their weapons were always at the ready. "Charlie" had proven that he had no respect for rest and recuperation.

The only luxury they had was a transistor radio that one of Danny's fellow Marines, Baker, owned. Baker was a big, tough African-American boy from Chicago. He had gold-capped teeth that shimmered even in the moonlight.

Baker could tune into the American Forces Vietnam Network (AFVN). The AFVN would broadcast the Vietnam military news, but what Danny and the boys were really interested in was the music. Some good ole Rock n' roll. It is amazing what Rock n' roll can do for the soul.

One day, a particular song got their attention as it vibrated through the little transistor radio's speaker. It was "Light My Fire" by the Doors. The lyrics seemed to take on a life of their own for these weary Marines.

You know that it would be untrue
You know that I would be a liar
If I was to say to you
Girl, we couldn't get much higher

Danny couldn't contain himself. He grabbed his helmet and began to pound out the beat along with the music. This very rare, light moment in Nam took him back to his drum playing days. In reality, how far back can you go when you are only nineteen years old? Sometimes, I think we forget that these were just kids fighting for our freedom.

Danny loved music, particularly this song. He had been a drummer in a rock band called *The New Generation*. As he beat on his helmet half a world away, his mind was on stage at a gig they played back home on the Marshall University Campus in West Virginia. *The New Generation* lead singer, Gary Patton, was bellowing out those famous lyrics:

Come on baby, light my fire
Come on baby, light my fire
Try to set the night on fire
The time to hesitate is through
No time to wallow in the mire
Try now we can only lose
And our love becomes a funeral pyre . . .

The rest of the Squad were on their feet now, and they were all singing and dancing. It felt good to release some stress — they

needed to let loose! Oh, how they needed it. The jungle had given so few moments like this. The aroma of sweet laughter seeped from the tent onto the compound as the sun headed to bed on a cool night on the edge of the enemy in Vietnam.

As the night drew on, Danny and the boys got to know each other a little better. A bond began to build between those young Marines. This was a very rare occurrence in the jungles of Southeast Asia. For the most part, soldiers kept to themselves. No attachments, no worries, no mourning. But with this band of brothers, it was different.

Nicknames were given to the four men of Fire Team #1. If you didn't like yours, then that was tough because it was now branded on you for the rest of the war. Nicknames that had already started unofficially became official. Danny became *Dan Bo* and Sotere was *the Greek*. Philadelphia native Nick was now *Combat* and Wells from Arkansas was — well, he was still Wells.

It felt good to Danny. Dan Bo, the Greek, Combat, and Wells were now accepted by the more experienced Marines. Their uniforms had lost that department-store newness, fading and taking on the inescapable jungle grime and blood. Their boots were muddy, faded, and well-worn. But, it was their eyes that gave them the most respect from their fellow Marines. Their eyes told the story of experience, horror, and numbness.

There were two things the Marines looked forward to, mail and cold beer. When the mail runner came around with mail from the world, meaning the U.S., the Marines would eagerly anticipate getting some news from home or maybe even a care package from a relative.

Danny and Sotere hadn't been in Nam long enough to receive any mail. Danny thought to himself, "Who would I receive mail from anyway? Not many people know that I am over here, I don't have a girlfriend, and I'm not that close to my family outside of my grandmother." So, at this time, mail wasn't in the picture for Dan Bo or the Greek — but there *was* some cold beer.

At that moment, Corporal Kessler came into the tent holding a box of Budweiser. A little grin creased the sides of his mouth. "Anyone thirsty?" The tent erupted into whoops, hollers, and even a standing ovation for their illustrious leader.

"Now that is what I am talking about," shouted the Greek.

After the cans were passed out to everyone, Corporal Kessler held his can up high and said, "To the 3/5 First Squad — get some!" The tent erupted again into cheers.

"Men," continued Corporal Kessler, "Let's honor our fallen with a word of prayer. Bow your heads." The Marines did as they were told.

"God in Heaven, may You be with the souls of the brothers we lost in the last couple of weeks. They were heroes and paid the ultimate sacrifice. We pray that You would bring comfort and peace to their families.

"Please watch over us and protect us on our next mission. We know You made Marines to protect the world from evil such as the one we battle here. In Jesus' Name, we pray."

Altogether, the Marines in that tiny tent said, "Amen."

The Corporal looked up at his men and said, "I heard that we are going on our next op real soon. So, live, laugh, and get some rest!"

While the thought of going back out into the jungle brought a damper to the little party, Baker cranked up the radio. Wells yelled, "Now, it's time to party!"

That night was a bonding night for the First Squad. Music helped relax away the stress — at least for a little while. At one point during the evening, Sotere reached into his pocket, pulled out a picture of his girlfriend, Sophia, and gazed at her affectionately. You can imagine the ribbing he took from his comrades.

But Sotere didn't care. He loved Sophia and couldn't wait to get back home to her. Sophia was a beautiful Greek girl who adored Sotere. She lived back in his hometown of Cleveland. Gazing at the picture, he said softly, "Sophia, I'm going to marry you someday, my love." He then gave the photograph a gentle kiss and softly put it back into his pocket.

As the party was winding down and the Marines were turning in for the night, Danny felt a wave of melancholy come over him. He thought about how he hoped he would have someone like Sophia in his life someday.

In reality, his life was empty. Danny had been homeless and on his own since he was fourteen years old. Can you imagine being fourteen, and having to be totally responsible for your own well-being? Sure, it hadn't always been that way. Earlier, he had lived with a man named Oliver Lane. Oliver had adopted Danny, and for some time life was sort of normal.

Oliver was a tough, hard-nosed former Marine who demanded discipline. But Danny knew that Oliver loved him and only wanted the best for him. Oliver was also a cop. One day, tragedy hit Danny's life once again. It was two days before Christmas, 1963. Around 7:30 in the morning Danny heard some noise outside. Oliver had worked the night shift and was just getting home with some of his buddies from the police force. They were clearly in the holiday spirit, if you know what I mean. They were cracking jokes and shooting off their guns.

Danny ran outside to see what was going on. After a few more drinks and a handful more gunshots into the air, the other officers got in the car and drove away. Oliver put his hand on Danny's shoulder, smiled, and walked with his son back into their modest log cabin home.

Upon reaching the doorway, Oliver suddenly collapsed and fell face down. He was dead before he hit the ground. Danny screamed for help, but it was too late. The image of his adopted dad lying on the floor lifeless would haunt Danny for many years to come. After the funeral, a man came up to Danny and said, "Son, this was Oliver's .38 caliber revolver. Here, Oliver would have wanted you to have this." Little did Danny know that he would wear that same pistol on his own side as a police officer seven years later.

As all those images and memories flooded through his mind, the distant sound of artillery and gunfire brought him back to the here and now. He was in Nam, and that was that. There was no way out, unless severely wounded or in a body bag. He was exhausted, both physically and emotionally, and had only been in the country for three weeks. Three long, horrible weeks. Could it get any worse? If he had known what was to come, he wouldn't have asked that question.

CHAPTER THREE

OPERATION TAYLOR COMMON: ARIZONA TERRITORY

TWO MEDICAL TECHS ROLLED A GURNEY INTO Danny's room. "Are you Mr. Lane?" Danny glanced towards the door but gave no response. He had no idea it was 2006 and he was back in Huntington, WV.

"We need to know your name," said one of the techs. "Are you Danny Lane?" Again, there was no response from Danny.

The frustrated tech sighed heavily, walked briskly over to Danny's bedside and not so gently grabbed Danny's wrist and twisted it over to check the name bracelet. Satisfied, the tech began to unplug the IV and EKG chords.

A couple of minutes later, the techs had Danny stretched out on the gurney, and the trio headed towards the MRI unit. Once inside the unit, one of the techs said, "Mr. Lane, this is the MRI unit. We are going to do some scans of your brain. You will be in the tube for 45 minutes. Now, here is a button. If, for any reason, you feel that you can't handle it anymore and need to come out of the tube, then press that button, and I will bring you out. Do you understand?" Danny said nothing, but did accept the button when the tech handed it to him.

"Mr. Lane, I will be talking with you and monitoring you throughout the exam. You will be fine in the tube. You are going to hear some loud bangs throughout the examination. This is normal. You also need to lay as still as possible. Do you understand Mr. Lane?" Again, no response.

As the belt slowly moved Danny into the tube, his fingers slightly tightened around the button the tech had given him. After about 15 minutes of scanning, the jackhammer bangs started to rumble in Danny's ears and body. Panic began to envelop him, and his mind raced back to the dark tunnels the enemy hid in during the war. Danny and his fellow Marines had to clear out those dark, dangerous underground holes. The loud booms of the MRI machine resembled the explosions that were a constant in Vietnam. To Danny's scrambled mind, he was back in Southeast Asia. Danny's breath began to shorten and his heart began to race. He pushed the button in his right hand repeatedly.

The tech responded calmly over the microphone, "Mr. Lane? Are you ok?"

"Retreat! Retreat! PULL BACK — NOW!" yelled Danny.

"Mr. Lane, if I pull you out now we will have to start the test all over again," said the frustrated tech. "Danny, are you hearing me?"

"Retreat! PULL BACK — NOW!"

The tech looked at his counterpart and said, "Get him out of there. He is making no sense at all."

After Danny was out of the tube, the tech glared at him and said curtly, "Now, you will have to take the entire test all over again. What a waste of time!"

Danny looked at him and said, "Screw you!"

"Fine," said the tech. "If that is the way you want it." He motioned to the door and said to his counterpart, "Get him out of here. Get him back to his room."

As the other tech escorted Danny out the door, a yell came from behind them, "Vietnam Vets — they are all nuts!"

FIRE TEAM #1'S reprieve at An Hoa didn't last long. On December 10, 1968, their new orders arrived. The Marine companies gathered together for a briefing. Colonel Atkinson, the Battalion Commander, stepped to the front and paused to look over his Marines. He then said, "Men, we have new orders. Operation Taylor Common commenced three days ago. We are now going to join that fight. Our main objective is to take out the enemy stronghold designated Base Area 112. In order to do that, we will seek out the enemy wherever those cowards are hiding and clear a path to Base Area 112. Further details will be dispersed down the chain of command. Alright, let's move out!"

The main objective of Operation Taylor Common was to attack and cut off the enemy base identified as Base Area 112. It was to be a massive operation that would last three to four months.

Base Area 112 was a source of numerous attacks on the Americans. It was believed to be the support base for the enemy's NVA 21st Regiment, 3rd Battalion, 68B Rocket Regiment, 2nd Battalion, and 141st Regiment. Many rockets, mortar, and ground attacks on Da Nang and An Hoa drew their lifeblood from Base Area 112.

One of the targets, Da Nang, was the second largest city in South Vietnam and the home of the Marine 1st Division Command. Base Area 112 needed to be dealt with as swiftly as possible.

The enemy had positioned their base in the very rugged mountains southwest of An Hoa. Base Area 112 was located in the south-central coastal region of Vietnam in the Quang Nam Province. This province was vast and spread out all the way to the border of the neighboring nation of Laos. Once you crossed the river, you entered a literal hell on earth. The Americans nicknamed this land mass the "Arizona Territory."

In this region, the Marines were given rules of engagement equivalent to a "free fire zone." That meant that if any Marine came across someone who was of military age and not a Marine, he could kill them if they presented a credible threat. It sounds harsh, doesn't it? But, we have to remember the insidious strategies the enemy was using against our boys. An old man, or even an old woman, weren't necessarily what they appeared. The Marines learned this the hard way. More Americans died in this region than in any other area during the war. Over 58,000 Americans died in Vietnam, 14,000 of which were Marines. Approximately 10,000 of those Marines were killed in the "Arizona Territory."

American intelligence had revealed that the NVA were moving thousands of fresh troops and their accompaniment of support weaponry south from Hanoi in North Vietnam, through Laos, and into South Vietnam. These were not only fresh troops but seasoned troops. Danny and his comrades were now going against the best the enemy had at their disposal. Some of these elite enemy troops could be twice the age of our young Marines, and a hundred times more experienced.

In a nutshell, Operation Taylor Common was a search and destroy mission. It was conducted by Task Force Yankee, which was a task force comprised of soldiers from the 1st Marine Division with support from South Vietnam allies, the Army of the Republic of Vietnam (ARVN).

Operation Taylor Common had three phases of engagement. In **phase one**, Task Force Yankee would engage in clearing out operations from what was known as "Liberty Bridge," south to An Hoa. This terrain was in the lowlands and had a lot of rice paddies, rivers, small streams, and very dense jungle vegetation. The objective was to hunt out Charlie and destroy him. This had to be done on foot, inch by inch.

The greatest threat to the Marines were the enemy booby traps, which were everywhere and nowhere at the same time. You could walk right over one and not know your life was spared by stepping an inch to the left instead of right on top of it. You had to assume the traps were everywhere. You walked where the Marine walked in front of you. Even then, you crept ever so cautiously. Every step taken was a risk to your life. Your next step could initiate a hidden bomb blowing off your leg and half of your right side or a barbaric trap of wooden whittled spears attached to a primitive swing up and forward mechanism that would stab your entire body. Primitive, yes, but effective and deadly.

Another threat in the lowlands was the snipers. The Viet Cong didn't operate large groups of troops in these areas, so they used sharp-shooting snipers and small bands of troops to harass and kill our Marines.

Phase two of Operation Taylor Common consisted of a series of what were called Fire Support Bases. Command chose strategic locations southwest of An Hoa that lay along the approach routes to Base Area 112. These Fire Support Bases were positioned on the mountain tops and consisted of a Marine Infantry Company and their support artillery of 105mm and 155mm howitzers, 106mm recoilless rifles, and a battery of 81mm mortars. Navy Seabee engineers, as well as a first aid station staffed with medics, also set up on location at these Fire Support Bases.

The **third phase** was to commence after Base Area 112 was cleared. It would consist of recon missions further west toward Laos to prohibit the enemy troops and supplies from infiltrating from North Vietnam.

Another thing the Marines had to be aware of during Operation Taylor Common, as well as throughout the war, was that the enemy had an extensive underground tunnel system that they had built. The Viet Cong and North Vietnamese Army would house entire divisions in these tunnels. The tunnels were large and had living quarters, a kitchen, sleeping quarters, ammo dumps, and even a hospital for their wounded. It was amazing. The enemy was like a bunch of rats that would pop up out of nowhere to kill Marines. Then, as if disappearing with the clearing smoke, they would be gone. All that was left were Marines gathering their faculties and caring for their casualties. Danny and his fellow Marines were instructed to extensively hunt for the entry points to these tunnels and destroy them before the "rats" could come out of their holes.

To the troops, Operation Taylor Common seemed like some grandiose master plan created by the commanders in some far-off conference room as they sat around an oval mahogany table. Well, the truth is that wherever they created this master plan, and however it was done, most of it went over the heads of the grunts.

But Danny and his fellow grunts knew it was up to them to make the mission a success — or die trying. They were the foot soldiers who would very shortly be trudging in the rice paddies and dodging bullets from the tunnel rats. This time, however, they would be asked to use guerilla warfare against the masters of guerilla warfare, the North Vietnamese Army. But grunts go where they are told to go and do what they are told to do. They are Marines. "Semper Fideles" . . . "Always Faithful."

It was time to rock and roll; the mission had begun. It was early dawn on December 11, 1968, and it was already hot. The monsoons had tempered their fury, and now Vietnam was covered in thick humidity and raging temperatures nearing the century mark during the heat of the day.

The boys of Fire Team #1 stood ready on the tarmac in full combat gear with only two days' rest coming off Operation Meade River. Now it was time to go back to work.

Danny wiped some sweat off his already grimy brow. As he did, his hand bumped his helmet. He reached up and adjusted it snugly against his scalp. He looked over at the Greek standing next to him. As they locked eyes, an understanding flowed between them that only combat soldiers can begin to understand. On the other side of Danny stood Wells and Combat. Fire Team #1 was ready.

All four of them wore a different face than just a short three weeks earlier. They didn't wear the petrified face of a boot anymore. Their faces were hardened, firm, and resolute. By no means were they looking forward to what lay before them, but they were ready. They were grunts. They had seen combat. They had withstood the blood and death and had escaped on the other side. Now, in the depths of their own minds, they all had the same thought — could they cheat death again?

In the near distance, a low rumble could be heard from the massive engines of the CH-46 helicopters. As they soared over the rice paddies, a small ripple along the water surface shimmered ever so slightly. Danny knew that was their ride to the Arizona Territory. The massive machines sat down gently on the warm tarmac like a giant eagle resting upon its nest. Danny and the Marines boarded the craft and were back in the air in formation.

Fire Team #1 and many other Marines sat upon their helmets. They didn't have to be told this time around — and certainly didn't have to be reminded. The mood in the craft was somber, yet confident. They had experience with them this time. That experience also came with a heavy burden. They knew, without a shadow of a doubt that in a few short minutes some of them — maybe all of them — could be dead.

The helicopters soared in the direction of Liberty Bridge, which was about twenty miles from Da Nang near the Arizona Territory. Liberty Bridge was of utmost importance to the Americans. It was a vital link so that military vehicles could bring supplies to the Marines across the Thu Bon River. The bridge itself was 2,040 feet long and stood 35 feet above the surface of the Thu Bon River.

The helicopters descended toward the landing zone. Blades of grass waved violently from the assault of the manufactured wind from the chopper's rotor blades. Danny and his comrades quickly jumped out, expecting the worst.

Danny's thoughts went back to his introduction to combat three weeks earlier. On that day, Danny and Greek had met heavy resistance as they exited the helicopter. On this day, there was none — a pleasant, yet puzzling experience for the Marines. Like a dangerous game of hide and seek, quietness concerns the Marine.

3/5 Third Battalion Fifth Marines and its five companies had entered the lion's den. Each company consisted of about one hundred Marines. They were assigned to hunt out the enemy, destroy him, clear a path to the ultimate objective of Base Area 112, and obliterate it.

The Marine company quickly organized themselves and humped in the direction of their objective. The sweat poured off them. Inch by inch they moved as quickly as they could. Danny walked in the footsteps of the Marine ahead of him. The enemy booby traps were always on the Marines' minds. One wrong step and you were dead. One right step, in the wrong place, and you were also dead.

After some time, they came across a rice paddy. The mucky, murky water was not inviting. Danny forced himself to step forward, and his boot pierced the water's surface. He felt his boot sink into the soft bed. He glanced over at the villagers that were harvesting the rice paddy for their food. As he did, he locked eyes with an old woman holding a basket.

Danny hated the thought that now crossed his mind, "Is that really an old woman? She could be the enemy. The enemy sometimes disguises themselves as villagers, even women. This was a free fire zone but unless someone attacks you have to stand down. Even so, Danny's instincts and senses were on high alert.

Trudging through rice paddy dikes, swollen streams, and dense tree lines was already an exhausting duty. Then, try that with one hundred pounds of equipment hanging on your body.

The typical Marine's backpack and utility belt consisted of hundreds of rounds of extra ammunition, C-Rations of food that could last three to four days, a poncho, dry socks, rifle cleaning kit, ammo for the M-60 machine gun, an entrenching tool, four to six grenades, a compass, map, four canteens full of water, and a few personal items including the Bible.

On that first day, the Marines humped about five clicks without resistance. One click is about six-tenths of a mile. They then dug in for the night. An infantry company forms a circular perimeter at night in order to protect the command center. It was similar to how the old wagon trains would set up their camps at night as Americans moved westward 150 years ago. In those days, they were protecting themselves from Native American attacks and wild animals. In Vietnam, the concern was from Viet Cong sappers and tunnel rats who could spring up out of seemingly nowhere.

They positioned the makeshift command post in the center; then the Fire Teams dug foxholes for the night all around the perimeter. Each foxhole was about 20 yards apart and manned by a four-man Fire Team. This created a shield of protection for the officers and support staff.

Sleeping in a foxhole is not like sleeping at the Holiday Inn. In order to make it a bit more hospitable — or at least from the elements — Fire Team #1 joined all their ponchos together and created something that had the resemblance of a tent that they pitched near their foxhole. If they were lucky, there wouldn't be too many gaps that would let in the incessant rain.

The Regiment's mission was to become a blocking force for their South Vietnamese allies (ARVN Rangers). The ARVN Rangers were to sweep the Viet Cong and the North Vietnamese Army towards them. Now, what made this so difficult was that the enemy very rarely moved during the day. When the sun was up, they either could be found concealed in the jungle canopy, or below your feet in the tunnels. This made blocking them very difficult.

The Marines knew the enemy was close. Charlie was probably watching them at that very moment. Danny could feel the enemy even though it was unseen. Have you ever felt someone watching you? That disturbing tingle on the back of your neck? That was an unnerving constancy in Vietnam. The air was always thick with danger. It put your senses on high alert and sent adrenaline pumping through your veins — it was like a constant IV drip that you couldn't shut off. It was time to shut it off by shutting down the enemy. It was time to find them and drag them out of their holes.

The Commanding Officer ordered the patrols to cover the canopy inch by inch, step by step, moving southward towards An Hoa. The platoons spread out in different directions in search of this communist plague that had infected the countryside. The elusive enemy would only be able to hide for so long.

Fire Team #1 walked the left flank, staying about 50 yards from the main Company to protect its left side. Danny marched up front on point. Being the Point Man was the most dangerous job in the infantry. With so many hidden ways to be killed, the Point Man had to know what to look for in and amongst the jungle vegetation. His life depended on it — not to mention the Marines walking directly behind him.

As Danny trudged through the dense vegetation, he ever so gently pushed a probe stick into the ground, looking for booby traps. The enemy troops were masters of concealment, so to keep your legs attached to your body, the Marine had to find the booby traps before they found him.

What Danny had learned at the 59-day Infantry Training Battalion (ITB) seemed to be a little less than adequate when trying to find hidden booby traps in the bush. But then, training can only do so much. Experience is the name of the game. But, how do you gain experience without getting yourself blown up in the process of gaining that experience?

As Danny and his Fire Team walked the left flank, he got the feeling that they were exposed like a raw nerve. As they made progress inch by inch, his thoughts went back to those days at ITB.

Before arriving in Vietnam, Danny and other Marines had reported to Camp Pendleton on the West coast of the United States in San Diego County. Camp Pendleton had been established in 1942 to train Marines before sending them to battle the AXIS Powers in World War II.

At ITB, under the direction of Combat Instructors, Danny learned the following skills: superior marksmanship, patrolling techniques, the proper use of grenades, identifying and countering improvised explosive devices (such as some of the booby traps in Vietnam), as well as other useful techniques needed when in combat.

The Viet Cong and North Vietnamese Army had a disadvantage when fighting against the Americans: firepower. But they made up for it devastatingly with their ingenuity. Their use of booby traps was sheer genius, to the detriment of our Marines. Booby traps were not only used to cause American casualties but also to delay the movement of troops and equipment. In fact, the utter fear of booby traps was enough to slow down a Marine advance of ground troops to a snail's pace.

The enemy also used booby traps effectively in creating killing zones. Enemy snipers sat off in the distance waiting and watching to pick off the unsuspecting Marines. A sniper's bullet is never heard before it hits its target. That was a fear that was always in the back of Danny's mind, as well as the minds of all his fellow Marines.

Booby traps also had another long-term impact on the Marines, but that was not one of a physical nature. The long-term impact I am speaking of was one of a psychological nature. The

Marines in the field were under a constant state of high stress. This created severe mental fatigue that lasted long after the war was over — sometimes for a lifetime.

Just today, as I was watching the news, a veteran was being interviewed. The reporter was conducting the interview outside. As the interview commenced, a car backfired in the near distance. The former combat soldier reacted instinctively and immediately to the sound that was similar to mortar fire in Vietnam. Fortunately, the reporter had seen combat himself and was compassionate and understanding of our war hero.

It isn't delusional to say that the Viet Cong (VC) and the North Vietnamese Army (NVA) could kill a man in a hundred different ways. They were experts at taking anything, even someone else's discarded trash, and making it into a killing mechanism. They were very experienced. After all, their ancestors had been fighting wars for a thousand years. Death and destruction had become their way of life . . . and no one knew how to do it better.

So, as you can imagine, every step Danny took was well guarded and well thought out. Besides individual explosive devices and the deadly bungee pit with its razor-sharp bungee sticks, the most common booby trap employed by the enemy was the trip wire. This almost invisible wire could be stretched across a trail, or anywhere the enemy thought they might catch an unsuspecting prey. When the wire was tripped, an explosive device activated and caused almost certain death or dismemberment.

Searching for Charlie wasn't an easy task. As mentioned before, if Charlie didn't want to be found, then it was near impossible to find him. American spy planes could never locate enemy troop movements. That is almost unthinkable until you realize the extent the enemy was willing to go to accomplish their goals.

Remember the tunnels? This meticulous, dedicated, intelligent enemy dug a network of extensive tunnels that encompassed tens of thousands of miles. American military intelligence said that the tunnels ran from North Vietnam through Laos and down into South Vietnam.

It is almost unfathomable the length and breadth of this tunnel system. They were even known to move undetected military equipment as large as tanks, trucks, and artillery. So, moving troops undetected was a simple matter.

Besides living quarters, kitchen, ammo dump, and a hospital, some tunnels even had large theaters and music halls in order to give the weary VC and NVA soldiers a needed diversion from the war above.

The Americans relied heavily on aerial bombardment. Unlike World War II, this bombardment in Vietnam often failed to achieve its desired result. The more the Americans bombed, the further and longer the enemy went underground.

As the Point Man, Danny cautiously led the Greek, Wells, and Combat through the dense vegetation. At ITB, Danny had learned that the best way to find a booby trap was to look for the enemy markers. The Viet Cong placed visual markers pointing to their booby traps to protect their own troops. The trouble was the enemy knew what they were looking for, while Danny had to guess. Examples of the enemy markers could be an odd formation of sticks, a broken bush, or a dozen other ingenious and hidden clues.

Danny lifted his left foot about three inches off the ground, about to take another step. He paused ever so slightly and peered intently at the terrain in front of his dirt-caked, worn foot. The ground looked clean. No signs of tampering. He set his foot down and waited — nothing. He sighed in internal relief.

As they continued up the left flank, they could see a long line of Marines on their right, which was the main company. Beyond what he could see, Danny knew that a handful of mirror Marines were walking the right flank as they were walking the left.

A slight warm breeze creased the air. As it did, a loud explosion fractured the air about one hundred yards away. Instinctively, they all hit the ground. About five seconds passed, then someone yelled, "Corpsman Up!"

Danny could see a Navy Corpsman hurrying to the right flank. A Marine had found a booby trap in the way no one ever wanted to find them. The Marine's screams of pain and terror of death rang for all to hear. The corpsman arrived to find the Marine's leg was partially blown apart, and his body was riddled with shrapnel. For that Marine, the war was over and his life was changed forever.

The company stayed put until a Medivac helicopter arrived. After it set down, a handful of Marines picked up the wounded warrior and swiftly carried him and loaded him on the helicopter.

The helicopter lifted off and began to gain altitude. As it did, the company Commanding Officer yelled for all his troops to hear, "Be alert! Watch your every step! This place is crawling with those things! You don't want to be next!"

After several long hours of gruelingly moving through the bush, they came to an opening in the jungle canopy. The CO instructed them to set up a temporary perimeter. Danny set down his pack. It felt good to him to be relieved of that weight for a while — not to mention the weight of being the Point Man.

The Marines prepared to get some much-needed rest and some food to refuel their bodies. However, rest was not in the cards for Danny and the Greek. Corporal Kessler assigned them to set up a nearby daytime Observation Post (OP) about 100 yards from the Company.

The two took up their position near an old, abandoned bamboo hut. It felt good on their weary bones to sit down and eat some C-rations. It was a hot, sunny day; the kind of day where you would love to be on a beach with a good book. Well, with no beach in view and no library next door, the boys did the next best thing: Danny and the Greek lay back against the bamboo outside wall of the hut and relaxed.

At that moment, they heard a sound — it sounded like whispering. The boys instantly froze. What was that? Who was that? Danny alerted the Greek with a hand gesture, and quietly got back on his feet. As quiet as a cat on the prowl, he moved closer to the thick bamboo wall of the hut. With his rifle in his hand, Danny eased his ear up to the wall and strained to the edge of his hearing.

What he heard put a shiver through his entire body and shoved his stomach in his throat. Someone was speaking Vietnamese. No, not just one; there was a conversation going on. At least two people, maybe more.

Danny and the Greek quietly pulled apart the bamboo making up the wall and peeked in between the sticks. Hiding in their makeshift bamboo fortress were two VC soldiers squatting on the dry dirt floor. Beside them on the ground were their Russian-made AK-47 semi-automatic machine guns. In their hands, they each were holding a Chinese Communist grenade.

The enemy soldiers became aware that they were being watched. With senses alerted, they looked around and locked eyes with Danny and the Greek. An eternity passed as the four combatants were frozen in a soldier's stare. Danny and the Greek pointed their M-16 machine guns at the enemy soldiers.

"Greek, tell them to *surrender or die!*"

"Surrender or die," yelled the Greek. The VC just stared at him.

"No man, I mean in Vietnamese. Remember? They taught us that in training."

"H*lls bells, Danny. I barely know English. You expect me to remember that Vietnamese crap they taught us in training?"

"Well, tell them something," said Danny. "They've got grenades in their hands."

The Greek paused and looked up in thought. He then got a determined look and pulled out his .45 pistol. He raced across the hut and harshly pushed his piece between the eyes of one of the enemy combatants. He then began yelling in Greek, "Πάγωμα M F R ή θα φυσήξει σας F N αποκεφαλισμένοι! Págoma í tha bloiw to kefáli sas." The shocked VC slowly let the Chicom grenades slide off their fingertips and onto the dry dirt floor.

"Man, that worked," said Danny. "What did you say?"

"Something like 'drop the grenades mother f'er's or I'll blow your brains out.' Then I called them a few more colorful names."

Danny chuckled and swung his M-16 in an upward motion telling the two VC soldiers to get up. They understood immediately and began to slowly get on their feet. "Search em good, Greek."

"Yeah, I got them, Dan Bo," said the Greek. As Danny held his rifle on them, the Greek walked over to them and pressed down firmly on their shoulders, forcing them into a sitting position. He then forced them to put their hands on their heads.

When the prisoners were secure, Danny walked over and picked up the grenades. He scrutinized them very carefully to make sure they were safe. Danny and the Greek then marched the POW VCs back towards the command center. It is hard to describe the feeling that Danny and the Greek felt as they paraded their prisoners back through the Marine camp. It was part humble pride, part confidence, and part relief.

As the odd quartet walked through the camp, Marines looked up from their current duties or from grabbing a quick meal to watch the spectacle. The CO walked up with a sly smile on his face and said, "What do we have here, ladies? Some little gooks, huh?"

"Yes, Sir," said Danny.

"Where did you find them?"

"In the bamboo, Sir," said the Greek, pointing in the direction from which they had just come. "There is a makeshift hut over there."

"Good job men," said the CO. That is the first time that Danny could recall their Commanding Officer ever calling him and the Greek "men." Usually, it was "ladies." The change felt good — really good!

The CO called over the South Vietnamese Ranger who was assigned to their unit. The Ranger began interrogating the two POWs, attempting to gather information about their base camp, unit, and other military data. As expected, the POWs gave up nothing. The Ranger then progressed to, let me say, some more open-handed tactics in extracting the information from the enemy, but it was to no avail as well.

Now livid, the South Vietnamese Ranger called in a helicopter for the POWs. After some heavy language and some more manhandling, he and the POWs were aboard the helicopter.

Once airborne, the helicopter circled over the camp for quite some time. Danny wondered what they were doing. Then, up around a thousand feet or so, Danny could make out in the distance what looked like a body soaring out of the helicopter.

"Man, did you see that?" exclaimed the Greek.

"Yeah. I bet he wished he had talked now," said Danny. Standing next to Danny, Wells and Combat shook their heads in disbelief.

Not long after, the helicopter landed and out bounded the South Vietnamese Ranger. The helicopter then took off with the one surviving prisoner and flew into the distance. He then walked briskly up to the CO and briefed him on what took place in the air. This interrogation technique used by our South Vietnamese ally makes the waterboarding of today seem kind of mild, doesn't it?

Danny and the other Marines looked at each other but said nothing; they knew better. The incident in the air was never discussed again. Were they shocked by it? Of course. But, they never questioned it. This was WAR! The South Vietnamese Ranger was sending a clear message to all who saw it — both enemy and ally alike. This was his country. It was being invaded by a plague from the north and he would spare no lengths to take his country back.

The South Vietnamese Ranger then informed the Marines that there was an NVA Command and Support Center directly below their feet in a massive tunnel. His technique was barbaric and inhumane, but he got the information out of one of the captured soldiers.

Now the Marines went on a massive search of the surrounding area to discover the entrance to the tunnel. Fire Team #1 began searching the vegetation around the camp. "I think I got something," said Danny.

The Greek came over next to his friend and began examining the area too. The foliage looked suspicious. It could be the entrance they were seeking, or it might be a booby trap — or maybe nothing at all. Either way, extreme caution was in order. After some careful moving of the jungle vegetation, they discovered it was a false alarm.

However, some yards away, Wells yelled, "I have found it!" Sure enough, it was the entrance to the tunnel. The entrance, more like a hole, was very small. The entrance had been expertly camouflaged with bamboo and jungle foliage. One could have walked over it a thousand times, and probably did, without ever knowing it was there. So small was the tunnel entrance that only the smallest of Marines could navigate their body into such a tight space. These American tunnel rats would be the first into the enemy lair, and many times go in unaccompanied.

In Kessler's squad, that honor went to Rootie Poot. Rootie was a member of Fire Team #2. He had curly brown hair and just a glimpse of peach fuzz on his dirt-speckled face. He was small in stature. He came in at just 5 feet, 6 inches tall — that is if he stretched himself up to his full height with proper posture like his grandmother used to like to see. Soaking wet, he weighed only 135 pounds. So Rootie was the perfect guy for this illustrious assignment.

Rootie got down on all fours and slowly peeked into the dark hole. He looked over his shoulder and locked eyes with Kessler. Kessler nodded ever so slightly to give him not only the go-ahead but encouragement as well. Rootie was scared, and can you blame him? He was being asked to enter the enemy's lair by himself.

Rootie turned back toward the hole. As he did, his right hand gripped the .45 caliber pistol tightly. In his left hand, he held a flashlight. Rootie eased himself into the small tunnel that led underground. Boy, it was dark — Rootie couldn't see his hand in front of his face. He held up the flashlight. The beam quivered just a bit as his heart began to race. All of a sudden, Rootie quickly pulled himself up out of the hole.

"I saw something!" he said.

"What was it?" asked Kessler.

"I don't know. But, I saw movement."

"Alright. Let's throw a gas grenade in there and see if we can clear out the entryway." Kessler then motioned to a Marine to get a gas grenade for Rootie.

Rootie crawled back inside the hole. He got in just far enough and pulled the pin on the grenade, activating it. He tossed it as far as he could in the cramped surroundings, then as quick as he could he scrambled up and out of the hole.

The Marines waited with bated breath. Nothing. Nothing at all. I am not sure what they expected to happen. Would the enemy come out of their den? Would they hear the Viet Cong coughing? Would the enemy just give up?

After a few minutes, Kessler gave Rootie the nod to go back in. The gas would have dissipated enough that it would not harm Rootie. Rootie climbed back in the hole and disappeared. He was gone for several minutes. For Danny and the other Marines up on top of the ground, it felt like an eternity. I can only imagine what it felt like for Rootie.

Finally, Rootie popped his head up out of the hole. At the sign of the movement, the Marines instinctively lifted their weapons in Rootie's face. When realization came into focus, they all relaxed, and so did their weapons. Combat and Wells reached down and helped Rootie out of the hole.

"Well?" asked Kessler.

"It is absolutely huge," said an out-of-breath Rootie. "I saw no one down there. There are multiple passages that spread out like the fingers on a hand. The paths then head downward. Each channel leads to a large room."

"It must be permanent barracks for the Viet Cong," said Kessler. There usually are more than one entrance and exit to these tunnels, so we will disable this entrance and see what happens.

After a few moments of discussion, it was decided to use C-4 to blow it up. If there were enemy troops in that tunnel, then they couldn't be allowed to escape. And, it was too dangerous to send in more troops. So, C-4 was the answer. All Marines carry C-4 in their packs. C-4 is a putty type of explosive that feels similar to moist Playdough. Rootie went back into the hole with C-4 and a blasting cap enough to blow up a city block. After he had put the charges in place, he scrambled back out, pulling the detonation wire and switch as he did.

The Marines cleared the area and scrambled for cover. Kessler yelled, "Fire in the hole!" A second later the earth exploded. Pieces of dirt and foliage shot up and out, and some of the debris landed as far as fifty yards away. These Marines made sure that enemy lair would never be able to be used again.

The Marines then turned their attention forward and moved onto the next grid on the map. It was slow going because of all the rice paddies, fields, and streams that had to be navigated on this route.

Have you ever tried crossing a stream as deep as a small river with a hundred-pound pack on your back? It was tough going. And that was only half of the problem. As Danny came up and out of the water, he felt something on his right calf. He instinctively reached down to scratch and rub his leg. He felt something underneath his pants, just about 4 inches above the top of his boots. He lifted his pant leg and found an ugly, blood-sucking parasite. It was a leech, but it was a like a leech on steroids.

The leeches in Vietnam were absolutely huge. They were a reddish-brown color and would attach themselves to any exposed skin the Marine happened to have vacant. Many times, the skin didn't have to be exposed. They would slime their way into your pants, shirt, and even underneath your helmet. The leeches in Southeast Asia were attracted to Marines like a magnet is to steel. If I didn't know better, I would say those little bloodsuckers were working for the Viet Cong.

Danny reached down into his pack and pulled out a can of insect repellant. He sprayed it on the leech, and it began to loosen its grip just enough to where he could pull it off. When he did, a bloody mark was left on his lower leg, and gravity began to pull a slow stream of blood down his calf. It wasn't much blood, so Danny didn't even bother bandaging it. He simply pulled down his pant leg, picked up his pack, and continued hiking with the rest of the Marines. The leeches were a constant harassing companion for the Marines on these journeys through the bush. The only way to get them off of your skin was to use repellant as Danny did or to burn them off with a cigarette.

Being exhausted already made crossing the rice paddy dikes more than a challenge. For one thing, they were very narrow and muddied by the recent rain. The dikes were small stretches of dirt pushed up into a mound that stretched from one end of a rice field to the other. Many times, multiple fields butted up next to each other.

The Marines would walk on top of these dikes to cross the fields. The water on either side could sometimes be as deep as six feet. So, very carefully, the Marines inched themselves across these fields. Another problem was that when you were on the dike, you were very exposed to the enemy and even though you couldn't see them, you knew they were close by . . . watching.

Danny walked single file behind the Marines in front of him. His foot slipped on the muddy dike, but he seemed to regain his footing — until the weight of his hundred-pound pack shifted the balance — and into the water he went.

Being pulled down by his gear, Danny struggled with all of his might — that is, what was left of his already depleted energy — to get to the water's surface. His head cleared the boundary, and he sucked in air. In his next breath, he screamed, "Help!"

But, instead of a flurry of help from his comrades, he heard a cackle of laughs from some of the Marines. Danny struggled to get back onto the dike. It was nearly impossible. Can you imagine trying to lift yourself out of water that is over your head back onto a slippery surface when you are exhausted? How about with a hundred-pound pack on your back that weighs even more because it is soaking wet?

Danny went under again. Reaching the surface again and gasping for air, the thought crossed his mind that he could die in this field. Had he made it through horrendous battles just to die in a rice paddy? Really? Had it come to that?

As he was about to go under for the third time, help finally arrived. It was the Greek. Who else would come to his aid but his brother in arms? The Greek outstretched his hand. Danny grabbed it like a leech on open skin; there was no letting go. With

Danny now secure in the Greek's grip, Wells and Combat each grabbed an armpit and hauled Danny back up onto the dike.

Wet, embarrassed, and exhausted, Danny stated matter-of-factly, "It is about time! How many times did I have to go under before you all figured out I was drowning?"

With a sly grin, the Greek said, "Ah, Dan Bo, you know we wouldn't let you drown. Brother, we got more gooks to kill to save this here country."

There was solidarity among these four men. Danny was not only grateful that they had saved his life, but he was also grateful that they were with him as they walked this journey of hell known as Vietnam.

They helped Danny to his feet and continued toward the objective. The next two weeks were about the same as the two before. The Marines kept tightening the noose around the enemy's leathery neck at Base Area 112. Kessler's squad destroyed several enemy base camps, prison camps, enemy strategic fighting positions, and even a hospital. All of these had been abandoned before the Marines had arrived, but they made sure the enemy wouldn't be able to use them again.

Engagements with Charlie were few. The enemy wasn't looking for a fight. They mostly had bugged out towards the west, just leaving a token of troops behind to harass the advance of the Marines.

THE SUN was up and shining on this crisp October morning. Danny squinted as the sunshine streamed through his window at St. Mary's hospital.

A sound grabbed his attention as the door swung open and a man entered the room. Danny slowly turned over flat on his back and moved his head slowly to face the door. "Mr. Lane, this is Dr. McComas. I heard you had some difficulty during the MRI test. Don't worry; we will find other options. I heard you were able to communicate with the technicians though. That is a good sign."

At that moment, Danny's son Chris walked into the room. Under his arm, he carried a folder of documents, photographs, and magazines. "How is he doing today doctor?" asked a concerned Chris.

"Well, he couldn't stay in the MRI tube long enough to complete the scans, so I am going to have to find another way to get the needed information."

"What do you see are the other options?" asked Chris.

"Well, with a spinal tap through his back we can get brain fluid which we can test for viruses like meningitis. We can also check for other brain infections. I am going to order the spinal tap soon. My main concern is that it is very painful and I am not sure he can endure it in his current mental condition."

Chris looked at the doctor and said confidently, "Dad has been through a tremendous amount of pain in his life. I am sure he can endure this test."

"I hope you are right, because the only other option is to put him to sleep and then take the tests. I would rather not do that if I don't have to."

Holding up the folder, Chris said, "I brought some pictures of him and me and his other kids to see if he remembers us. For the last week, he hasn't been making much sense and has kind of been talking out of his head. Every night when it gets dark, he gets paranoid and freaks out. It has kind of scared me."

With compassion and sympathy in his eyes, Dr. McComas said, "Maybe his VA records will be able to shed some light on what is going on inside his mind. I expect them to arrive anytime."

"Thank you, doctor. I really appreciate all you are doing for my dad."

With that, Dr. McComas placed his hand on Chris' shoulder and gently squeezed. He then walked out of the room to give father and son some time alone. Chris walked over to the bedside and sat down next to Danny. "Hey, Dad! How are you doing today? I am your son — well, one of them anyway. Mark and Evan are your other sons, and Ashley and Alexa are your daughters. You and I live together. Do you remember me?"

Danny stared long and hard at the face beside his bedside. No images or memories came forth to his rescue. Dejected, but not losing resolve, Chris pulled out a handful of the photographs tucked neatly inside the folder on his lap. He held up a picture in front of Danny and said, "Look here. This is a picture of you and me with Chuck Norris. We were in Las Vegas. And here is another picture of us with Chuck at your karate school. Here is another one of you, Chuck, and Jean-Claude Van Damme working out. Do you remember Chuck Norris? You and he are good friends. He is a movie star." Holding up two more pictures Chris said, "Here is a picture of you as a Marine in Vietnam and one of you as a cop here in Huntington. Here you are on the cover of *Tae Kwon Do* and *Combat Magazine*."

Danny stared blankly at Chris and then at each of the pictures slowly. "Dad, I am going to leave these here with you so you can look at them," said Chris. "Hopefully, you will start to remember something." As Chris began to walk out the door, he turned and looked at his father holding two of the old photographs. Forcing down his emotions, Chris walked briskly out of the room.

CHAPTER FOUR

FIREBASE JAVELIN: BATTLING "THE BLOOD ROAD," MALARIA, AND GRENADE-THROWING ROCK APES

I T WAS NEW YEAR'S DAY, 1969, BUT THE CELEBRA-TION wasn't in Times Square in New York City and Danny wasn't holding a noisemaker — at least not of the fun variety. This celebration was in a place far, far from the Big Apple, in a jungle in Southeast Asia. One really couldn't call it a celebration, but the change of scenery was at least something.

On that day, Danny's company of Marines (the 3/5) was extracted from the lowlands of rice paddies and leeches to the more mountainous regions of Quang Nam, which were south-west of the enemy's Base Area 112. Their mission was to set up the Combat Operations Base, which was known as Firebase Javelin, or Hill 734. Marines also planned to set up two additional firebases — Firebase Tomahawk and Firebase Maxwell. These three firebases would be the launching point for the Marines' final showdown with the enemy at Base Area 112.

B-52 bombers had dropped enormous amounts of explosives on Hill 734 to soften it up before the Marines' arrival. The bomb-ers splintered the trees and cleared the canopy in order to create a landing zone for the transport helicopters.

When Danny and his comrades arrived, the helicopters set down ever so cautiously on top of the obliterated tree fragments and craters created by the bombing. Danny, the Greek, Wells, and Combat exited the chopper and began to take in their surroundings. At least they didn't have to worry about leeches for a while. The Marines' task was to secure the hill and hold that position, so that the Seabee engineers could bulldoze the hill into a command center.

The first thing the Marines had to do was prepare their defenses and make this jungle mountain their home away from home. They began by digging foxholes and positioning them in strategic fighting locations when the attacks would inevitably come. Each foxhole was lined with sandbags in order to provide more protection from the enemy bullets, rockets, and mortars.

Then, there was the rain. The incessant, wet, nasty rain. And when it wasn't raining, it was humid. There was always some form of moisture that had to be dealt with. They pitched their tents — stretched ponchos pretending to be tents — over the foxholes to provide some comfort from the rain. They used wooden ammo boxes for mattresses to keep off the saturated ground. They then surveyed their new home.

"It's not the Holiday Inn, but it's home," chuckled Combat.

"I wish we had a six pack and some 'wacky tobacky.' This crap is getting old," said Wells.

Fire Team #1 and the other Marines used machetes to clear away the dense canopy up to about twenty-five yards in front of their foxholes. This created a better "killing zone," so that Charlie would have a more difficult time sneaking up on them in the dark of night.

Fire Team #1 was loaded, to boot. Danny had an M-60 machine gun mounted on a tripod on top of the bunker, supported by sand bags. They had thousands of rounds of ammunition. They also had an M-79 grenade launcher; several M-16 rifles;

45-caliber pistols; a shotgun; an abundance of Claymore mines, trip flares, and M-26 grenades; and, of course, their bayonets. The White House wished it was so secure.

Throughout the day, choppers brought in the artillery for the Command Center. They brought in a battery of 105 howitzers and 106 recoilless rifles. More troops arrived throughout the day, as well. By nightfall, Fire Base Javelin was ready for operation.

With that task completed, three Marine companies (Danny's 3/5 Mike Company, Kilo Company, and H&S Company) were to operate search-and-destroy missions against Base Area 112, coming from the west. They were also ordered to execute recon missions in the neighboring country of Laos, to put eyes on, if possible, the enemy's movement of troops and military equipment into South Vietnam via the Ho Chi Minh Trail.

The Ho Chi Minh Trail was an extensive network of roads and footpaths that linked North Vietnam to South Vietnam through the neighboring countries of Laos and Cambodia. It was a combination of truck routes and smaller paths used by bicycles and troops on foot. The trail even had some waterways. In all, it was an elaborate transportation strategy covering 16,000 kilometers (9,940 miles) of ground; used to sneak enemy troops and equipment into South Vietnam.

The trail, also known as "The Blood Road," was a major thorn in the Americans' side. At times, as many as 20,000 enemy soldiers a month followed this route into the heart of American-protected South Vietnam. Despite ferocious American air strikes, the NVA and Viet Cong smuggled over 1 million troops, and vast amounts of supplies, to the battlefields in the South. Thorn in the Americans' side? It was more like a dagger.

On January 2, 1969, Mike Company 3/5 arrived at Hill 734. Now the Americans had three companies to tighten the noose on the enemy's Base 112, and to engage the North Vietnamese Army in Laos.

As Danny looked across the valley from the mountaintop, he could see the eerie land of Laos. What made it so eerie? He knew the enemy was lurking there. Even though he couldn't see them, or confirm the intelligence reports, he could feel them.

Laos itself was at the bottom of the mountain and on the other side of a river that was the only buffer between Laos and Vietnam. Intelligence reports said that as many as four North Vietnamese Army (NVA) regiments were trying to infiltrate South Vietnam by crossing this river.

The next day, January 3, was a special day. It was Danny's birthday. He had now reached the landmark of his second decade; he was twenty years old. But there were no celebrations, no presents from home, no nothing... only the preparation for the inevitable encounter with Charlie. A birthday to forget, that was for sure — if it was even possible to forget.

Back around their foxhole, Fire Team #1 surprised Danny with a little birthday celebration. The Greek had a small pound cake which came in his B-2 C-Ration Kit. He placed a bamboo stick in the middle of it and lit it with his lighter.

"Ah, happy birthday, Dan Bo," said the Greek. He then led Combat and Wells in their own rendition of the *Happy Birthday* song. Their singing would never win a Grammy, but it did make Danny smile.

"How old are you, Dan Bo?" asked Combat.

"Twenty. I'm not a kid."

"And still not old enough to shave," laughed Wells.

"You just wish you had a baby-smooth complexion like me," jested Danny. "Seriously, guys, this means a lot. Thank you."

"A toast," said the Greek, holding up his canteen. The others lifted theirs as well. The Greek continued, "To Dan Bo: one heck of a Marine who is, as they say, a lean, mean, fighting machine. Hip hip hooray!"

Now that Fire Base Javelin was up and operating, the Americans started a massive bombardment of the mountain top designated Hill 508. The goal was to soften up the region so that another fire base, Fire Base Maxwell, could be implemented even nearer to the enemy's Base Area 112.

After softening up the region, the 1st Marine Division Command thought it was secure enough to land Marines on the ground to take the hill. However, it didn't work out as planned. Upon landing, the 3rd Marines took on a great amount of hostile fire and had to vacate the area to a safe distance a few clicks from the hill. Many Marines lost their lives in that attempt. That set the stage for a ferocious jungle assault that lasted twelve days . . . until finally, the Americans took Hill 508. After great sacrifice, Fire Base Maxwell was now in place. The enemy stronghold of Base Area 112 had limited days left. The Americans were going to see to that.

For the next few weeks, Mike and Kilo Companies went on daily patrols, working their way towards the enemy stronghold. Their objective was to set up other fire bases near the enemy to surround and smother their effectiveness. Understandably, when entering the region of the lion's den, the Americans were welcomed with heavy resistance from the dug-in NVA. Like a rat in a corner, the NVA were fighting for their lives.

Meanwhile, Danny, the Greek, Combat, and Wells maintained perimeter security at Fire Base Javelin to maintain the base's security. They went out on reconnaissance missions during the day, and ambush missions and perimeter security by night. Charlie would regularly keep the Marines on edge by launching mortar attacks and probes of the Marine lines.

Little did the Marines know that this was just the calm before the storm. Unbeknownst to them, at that very moment, four NVA divisions — totaling about twenty thousand men — were migrating from the north through Laos and heading south directly towards the Marines.

Can you imagine living on a jungle mountaintop day and night for what seemed like an eternity? Our war fighters in Vietnam had to deal with so many challenges beyond the normal battles with the Viet Cong and NVA. In fact, the challenges of the battlefield seemed almost simple in comparison to the many other elements facing them. Many Marines looked forward to the battles with the NVA because it relieved the anxiety of the other battles they faced constantly.

First, there was the weather itself. When it wasn't raining, it was incessantly hot. Outrageously hot. The humidity was so thick it was like taking a constant sweat bath as moisture poured off your body. Danny and his fellow Marines would have to hike for miles on patrol through a densely thick jungle canopy with hundred-pound packs on their backs. The temperature was so hot that they thought their brains would explode. As a result, they faced continual heat exhaustion, as well as deadly dehydration because of the lack of drinking water.

All this humidity and heat brought out mosquito swarms so thick you could wrap yourself in them like a blanket. The only problem was, this blanket gave you malaria and dysentery. Not something you want to cuddle up with on a warm summer's night.

The thick, razor-sharp elephant grass would rip lacerations in Danny's arms and legs, and many would eventually become sores that irritated him constantly as he tried to stay alive in this armpit of the world.

All the moisture the Marines faced through rain and humidity caused another problem . . . Jungle rot. Their feet were constantly wet, and it was nearly impossible to keep their socks and boots dry. As a result, the Marines faced jungle rot on their feet. Jungle rot is basically a tropical ulcer. Imagine lesions on your feet that cause tremendous pain; then imagine walking, not to mention fighting a war. If medical care was neglected for too long, these lesions could extend deeper into the muscles and tendons, and eventually reach the bones. That could lead to amputation.

Now, that was just the challenges caused by the weather. Danny and the Marines also had to deal with the bugs. Armies of bugs. Besides the already-mentioned mosquitos, our warriors also had to battle fire ants. Named partially for their red color, the fire ants were also known for their painful, fire-like sting. Then there were the poisonous centipedes and, last but not least, scorpions.

But all the old Vietnam War-era movies show the rats. Were there rats? Oh, yeah, there were rats — lots of the dirty, ugly, nasty varmints. On top of that, there were snakes; about 140 different species of snakes, to be exact. Now, don't worry, only about thirty of those species were poisonous. Thirty species of poisonous snakes? You'd better believe it.

At night, the Marines were taught to lie perfectly still if they felt something crawling on their bodies. At best, the snake would think you were a hump of dirt and go on its merry way. At worst, it would be alerted that you weren't dirt and attack! On many occasions, Danny had these nasty creatures crawl over him during the middle of the night. That is why, if at all possible, he would try to sleep on top of an ammo crate. Those few inches off the ground can make a world of difference.

One of the strangest encounters Danny had to deal with was the crazy, grenade-throwing "rock apes." Yes, you read that correctly. The Viet Cong took great lengths to train the local jungle inhabitants to help them in their war effort. They trained these apes to attack our troops with rocks, sticks, and sometimes even with grenades.

How would you feel? You are lying in your foxhole, tense with fear, expecting the enemy to attack at any moment — and they don't disappoint you. But what is that coming? You can't quite make it out; the night is pitch black. You strain your eyes, knowing that the enemy only attacks at night . . . What is that? Is

that a man? It is about as tall as a man, and it is walking upright
. . . But it moves funny. The next thing you know, a grenade is
launched through the air towards your foxhole, and you're dead.

That is what our troops had to deal with in Southeast Asia.
Some legends say that the rock apes are descendants of the mythi-
cal Big Foot. Well, I wouldn't go that far, but they were certainly
an intimidating problem. They could move as silently as a cat,
but had the strength to crush your sleeping neck. They walked
upright, so they appeared as a man of short stature. Now, who
really trains an ape to do their dirty work? Well, the Viet Cong,
that is who. That was the kind of war that was being waged against
us in Vietnam.

On one particular night, Danny was sitting in his foxhole
waiting for the inevitable, when he heard something. It wasn't
much; it was more of a rustle. It might be nothing. He shifted the
weight of the huge M-60 machine gun that was resting on his lap.
He strained his eyes to see what was unseen in the darkness of the
Vietnam sky, and there it was: a rock ape. It was close — real close.
Then he saw what it was doing; it was urinating on the Greek. The
warm stream woke the Greek up with a jolt. "What the. . .?" the
Greek yelled.

In the split second that followed, a random thought crossed
Danny's mind: "Are you kidding me? That is gross." But then,
the realization made him angry. The Marines hated these crazy,
grenade throwing monsters of terror. "It is bad enough that they
throw sticks, rocks, and grenades at us. Now, they are peeing on
us!" thought Danny. Out of instinct, Danny lifted his M-60 and
let it rip. He blew that crazy ape into a thousand pieces of gut flying chunks soaring through the blue-black night sky. That was one
ape whose peeing days were over.

When the smoke had cleared, there stood the Greek with
a wet splotch on his side and ape chunks on his helmet. Danny
looked at him, and said with a grin, "You're welcome." Combat

and Wells laughed so hard that their sides hurt. That was one memory they never let the Greek forget.

Just then, the Marines in the surrounding foxholes opened fire in front of their position, thinking the enemy was attacking. Danny looked up and saw illumination grenades lighting up the night sky. He picked up the radio and said, "FT1 to Command."

"Go ahead, FT1."

"All clear here . . . False alarm, just a rock ape."

"Copy, FT1."

Probably the toughest part of living in Vietnam was the constant anxiety. There was never a break from it. Every day started and ended the same way — wondering if this would be your last day on earth.

The days were long, and the nights were even longer. Minutes passed into hours, hours into days, and days into weeks. The Marines got very little rest. It was a constant struggle to keep their senses sharp, but dull senses belonged to dead Marines.

The Marines lived on the side of that mountain in a poncho tent in a foxhole with sandbags all around it. There was no transistor radio, no telephone, no television, no contact with the outside world at all. After awhile, all the days seemed as unvaried as beige, and the Marines forgot what day of the week it was — let alone the actual date. There were no showers, no shaving, no hot meals, and not even clean or dry clothes. No reminder of civilized life remained; just a date with destiny where the Viet Cong was their dancing partner.

The nights were darker than the darkest Halloween night — so dark you couldn't have seen your hand eight centimeters in front of your face. It was totally silent except for the eerie jungle sounds and constant buzzing of mosquitos in your ears. You knew Charlie was nearby, but you had no idea where. There was the ever-present, real fear of the enemy crawling up to your foxhole and cutting your throat before you were ever aware of what had killed you. As a result, Danny and the Marines were afraid to make any sound that might advertise their position. So, they didn't talk, light a cigarette, sneeze, or even move. Even relieving themselves was not an option, and passing gas was out of the question. If the sound didn't alert Charlie, the smell would be like a beacon in the night sky.

On January 15, 1969, the Marines received news that sent a shock wave through the entire company. Their Regimental Commander, Colonel Michael M. Spark, was dead. Colonel Spark's helicopter had received automatic weapons fire during a reconnaissance mission near Firebase Javelin, and had gone down. The Fifth Marine Regiment burned with fury. The constant anxiety had been building up, and this news had just lit the fuse — it was payback time. An engagement with Charlie could not come soon enough.

For the next two weeks, Fire Team #1 joined Mike and Kilo Companies as they covered a twelve-mile sweep of the Laos border near Highway 14. It was a rough month. Six Marines from Kilo Company were lost to drowning while attempting to cross the Vu Gia River; the current was so strong that they never had a chance. They might have made it if it weren't for the hundred-pound packs on their backs. In that short, four-week span, Kilo Company had eight men killed in action and thirty wounded. Was it worth it to sweep this twelve-mile land area? I don't know, but they did capture some important Intel. They reported seeing Russian and Chinese troops sprinkled among the North Vietnamese Army. Vietnam was heating up!

As you can imagine, living in this state of anxiety all the time can be quite wearing on the soul. By early February, 1969, Fire Team #1 had been on this operation for more than two months. On a particularly miserable night, Fire Team #1 found itself on bunker watch duty. Wells and Combat had had enough, and they wanted a break. They *needed* a break. They were both very brave, courageous Marines who were fed up with the jungle life. So, they came up with an ingenious plan to win some R & R.

They planned to toss a live grenade about ten yards in front of their foxhole, and then stick their rear ends out towards the blast. They would make sure the rest of their bodies were covered by their flak jackets and helmets. Only the place where the sun don't shine would be exposed. Their warped thinking was that they would receive some shrapnel in their derrieres, and then be sent to Japan to recuperate.

Danny and the Greek thought they were nuts and wanted nothing to do with it. They knew that it was not only a foolish plan, but it could also get them into a lot of trouble. Not only could they get court marshaled and receive a dishonorable discharge — they could die doing something so stupid.

Some long minutes passed, and Danny was getting more and more fed up with Wells and Combat's constant bickering and back and forth on who was going to throw the grenade. So, Danny reached into his pack and pulled out one of his own M-26 grenades. He rolled it around in his hands.

At this point, this strange motion received rapt attention from Wells, Combat, and the Greek. Danny looked up at the three of them and, with a sly hint of a smile on the corners of his mouth, he pulled the pin.

Danny looked right at Wells and Combat and said, "Stick your butts in the air. You have exactly three seconds before they are blown off." He then tossed the grenade in front of the foxhole.

Let me tell you, that three seconds felt like 60 hours. One thousand, two thousand, three thousand . . . KA BOOM! All of a sudden, all Hades broke loose. The other Marines thought they were under attack. Illumination lights lit up the night sky as if it were daytime. Bullets started flying from the Marines' barrels to hold Charlie at bay — except there was no Charlie. After a few minutes, all was quiet.

All the foxholes had to check in with command. They could hear Marines yelling in the near distance, "All clear." Finally, it was their foxhole's turn to report in. Nobody said a word. They all stared into each other's eyes. After another second of eternity, Danny yelled, "All clear!"

Wells and Combat then began feverishly checking themselves all over. "You hit?" asked Combat.

"No. You?" asked Wells.

"No. Me neither."

They then looked at Danny and asked, "What the h*ll were you doing? Are you nuts?"

"Maybe so. Just tryin' to help you out. You guys said you wanted a vacation. If you two were going to be so stupid, I just thought I would take you the rest of the way."

The Greek just looked at them all and shook his head in disbelief. The four friends laughed and agreed that they would never bring this incident up again.

Wells and Combat were good Marines; they were just at a breaking point. The human mind can only endure so much trauma before thoughts of escape or suicide begin to seep insidiously into the human mind.

The statistics on this type of tragedy are staggering. The military archives show that there were 58,202 American casualties during the Vietnam War. However, of that 58,202, only 40,934 died of wounds suffered during combat. Many soldiers died from other causes such as accidental weapons fire, other mishaps, and illness. Over twelve hundred soldiers were declared dead with no explanation. But, two statistics get to me more than any others. First, 236 died because they were murdered by their own troops. Think about that for a moment. Aren't soldiers supposed to be brothers in arms? That is a nice thought for the movies, but it isn't always a reality. And on top of that, 382 soldiers died of self-inflicted wounds.

From November 20, 1968, to February 7, 1969, Danny and the Greek stayed in the bush with only four days' respite. It seemed like an eternity. In many ways, it was. They had served with honor and courage, and now Danny had to deal with another uncertainty. This time, it wasn't Charlie. This uncertainty and discomfort were caused by an ever-present pest, which infected Danny with a sickness he felt would never go away. A few weeks earlier, Danny had contracted malaria, spread by the swarms of mosquitos.

Even though the troops were given the serum to prevent malaria before landing in-country, this illness still caused tens of thousands of Americans to get sick during their time in Vietnam. To make matters worse, the troops couldn't wear mosquito repellent at night. It was strictly taboo. Why? Because Charlie would smell it and ID your position.

Danny had constant chills accompanied by a high fever. Think of the worst night sweats you have ever had in your life . . . and that isn't even close to what Danny experienced; not just at night, but all day long, too. He was so nauseated that he just wanted to go to sleep and not wake up. Danny was already thin, but malaria caused him to lose a tremendous amount of weight — to the point where he looked like a walking skeleton wearing the Marine green. To his credit, Danny stayed with his company all that time. He just sucked it up and did his job.

DR. MCCOMAS walked into Danny's room in St. Mary's ICU. "Mr. Lane, I am Dr. McComas. Do you remember me yet?" The doctor paused for a moment before continuing to see if Danny would respond. Unfortunately, there was still no response. Only a blank stare came from the man in the bed. A small frown creased the corners of Dr. McComas' mouth, then he continued,

"I received your Veterans Administration records today. They contain some very interesting things.

"Mr. Lane, you were in the Marine Corps from 1968 through 1974. You were in the infantry and saw quite a bit of combat in Vietnam in 1968 and 1969. You were wounded twice and received two Purple Hearts. For your valor, you also were awarded the Combat Action Medal and numerous other medals and unit citations. It appears you were a hero."

Shuffling through the pages in the report, Dr. McComas continued, "It looks like you took part in four major military operations. Let's see; you also contracted malaria, were exposed to Agent Orange, and contracted hepatitis. That last one was probably from drinking contaminated water in the jungle itself, or from the rice paddies."

"It looks like you also receive a Veteran's disability pension for the combat wounds you obtained, as well as Post Traumatic Stress Disorder. It looks like you have had an ongoing battle with Post Traumatic Stress Disorder since your return from Vietnam. They have had you on a ton a medication over the years. There are medicines listed here for depression, anxiety, sleep deprivation, and even mood swings. Mr. Lane, I am surprised you have been able to accomplish as much as you have in your life while dealing with all this — not to mention all the medication in your body."

Dr. McComas looked into Danny's blank eyes. Rubbing his chin, the doctor thought, "I wonder what is going on inside that brain of yours? Will we ever know?"

CHAPTER FIVE

SEA KNIGHT DOWN

ON FEBRUARY 13, 1969, THE MARINES SHUT DOWN their mountain hideaway of Firebase Javelin, which was near Laos, and prepared to take up residence at Firebase Tomahawk, which was closer to the enemy's Area Base 112. The noose was tightening, and the inevitable was right around the corner.

The troops and equipment were transported by helicopter because of the surrounding dense jungle canopy and the distance that had to be covered. Danny and Fire Team #1 hauled their weary bodies aboard a C-46 "Sea Knight" helicopter, which had just landed. Joining them on board was Fire Team #2, which consisted of team members Walker, Cohen, Tex, and Rootie Poot. Corporal Kessler and Fire Team #3 followed in the next helicopter.

As the big chopper carrying Fire Teams #1 and #2 lifted off the ground, all eight Marines immediately took off their helmets and sat upon them. Experience had taught them well. For a while, they sailed through the air for what seemed like a vacation tour over a scenic island. Experience had also taught them, however, that brief reprieves could be a mirage. Danger was always lurking in Vietnam. On that day, it was particularly true.

Out of the blue, Walker slumped over and fell off his helmet like a wino off his fruit crate in an abandoned alley. Danny rushed over to him to see what had happened, and discovered that Walker had been shot. A sniper's bullet had found its prey through the hull like a pencil point through a piece of paper.

"We have incoming," Danny yelled towards the cockpit. "Walker is down! Sniper!"

The door gunner began to scan the horizon for the sniper. He was looking for a reflection, or anything that might give away the enemy marksman's location. However, finding a sniper in the Vietnam jungle was like finding leftover food on a teenage boy's dinner plate; it is not going to happen.

The door gunner laid down a large spread of his own bullets, hoping luck would find his target. However, the luck went the wrong way. The door gunner slumped over his weapon, hit by the sniper's bullet.

Danny yelled to the pilots, "Gunner is hit too. Pull back! Pull back!"

The pilot mashed down on the left foot pedal and at the same time pulled upward on the lever with his right hand, banking the chopper skyward and towards the left . . . hopefully out of the sniper's range. But it was too little, too late. Bullets continued to penetrate the hull. One hit the fuel tank, and fuel began pouring out of the aircraft. Then matters went from awful to, well, no good at all. The fuel ignited, and flames began to leap up towards the aircraft.

"We are losing pressure and fuel," yelled the pilot, a Second Lieutenant just trying to survive to become a First Lieutenant. "We are going down. Prepare for a crash landing!"

The pilot then called into the radio, "Darkhorse, this is Dolphin 25. We are taking fire. Going down. Coordinates 15 degrees 44' 20.4" N, 107 degrees 48' 36" E. 15.739, 107.81."

"Copy, Dolphin 25. Help is on the way," responded Darkhorse.

The flaming C-46 began to spiral like a corkscrew toward the ground, which was coming closer by the second. Danny glanced over and locked eyes with the Greek — that glance said it all. Two brothers, though separated by birth and born to two different mothers, were bonded for life — a life which appeared to be near its end. Danny reached over and clasped his hand on the Greek's shoulder.

The pilot glanced over his shoulder toward the Marines and yelled, "This is it! Take crash positions!" The Marines didn't have to be told twice. They tucked their heads and braced for the impact.

A few seconds earlier, the pilot had spotted a nearby river and immediately turned the spiraling craft towards it the best he could. It wouldn't be a soft landing, but it would be better than the solid ground.

The helicopter hit the water at an angle and turned on its side. The spinning rotor blades splintered as they hit the river and flew off in all directions. The water put out the flaming engine, but that same water was raging into the hull and engulfing the Marines.

Danny and the Greek checked themselves for injuries, and surprisingly discovered that they weren't injured. They immediately sprang into action to see about their comrades. The gunner was dead, but Walker was still alive. All the rest were not seriously injured. They grabbed what they could, including Walker, and scrambled from the sinking craft.

The sound of ricocheting bullets clinked as Danny broke a window so they could exit the craft. "We have incoming! MOVE IT" said Danny. Danny stuck his M-16 out the broken window and began firing toward the incoming bullets. "Greek, get everyone out of here. I will cover you!"

"Yeah, get it done, Greek. We got this!" said Wells as he joined Danny at the window and began firing his own weapon.

"Alright! Thanks, gents!" said the Greek. "Combat, give me a hand here."

Combat and the Greek grabbed the dead body of the gunner and began dragging him out of the chopper. Meanwhile, Cohen, Tex, and Rootie Poot quickly hauled the injured Walker from the craft. The pilot and co-pilot managed to slip out the front doors of the wounded bird.

As the others exited, Danny moved over and took over the door gunner's position with the huge M-60 machine gun. He peppered the jungle, and pretty soon all was quiet. He and Wells had held off the assault, at least for now. However, it wouldn't take the enemy long to regroup.

Danny lifted the M-60 off its stand in the back of the chopper and hauled it, and some extra ammo, into the water. He and Wells made their way toward the shore.

The exhausted Marines gathered on the shore and formed a small perimeter to secure the area. The Greek knelt over Walker and stabilized his wound. He would live, but his leg was in bad shape. Walking was not an option; he would have to be carried out. The Marines would also have to haul the gunner's body. It would be slow going, but Marines don't leave a soldier behind, dead or alive.

A distinct sound began to come over the tree tops — it was the cavalry. They saw the rescue C-46 helicopter as it began to hover over the extraction point. Danny popped a red smoke grenade to pinpoint their location for the rescue pilots.

It became obvious very quickly that the jungle was too dense and the chopper couldn't land. The chopper began to take on sniper fire, and was forced to lift to a higher altitude and out of the firing zone. Rescue Plan A had failed. The Marines were now on their own to form their own Rescue Plan B.

"D**n!" yelled the pilot. "What are we going to do now?" After a few seconds, the pilot said, "It looks like Firebase Tomahawk is probably about ten clicks from our location." With a deep sigh, he continued, "It could take us two or three days to get there on foot — if we are lucky."

The pilot reached down, picked up an M-16, and began issuing orders to the Marines. However, the Marines did nothing, and just stared at the pilot. Exasperated and not understanding, the pilot yelled, "What's wrong? Let's go, guys!"

"What do ya mean, Lieutenant?" asked the Greek. "What do you mean 'what do ya mean?'" Staring intently at the Greek, the pilot stated, "Son, I am the highest rank soldier here. I'm a Second Lieutenant! That means I am in charge."

"Sir, how many firefights, ambushes, and ground battles have you been in?" Danny asks.

"None," stuttered the pilot looking sheepishly at Danny. "With all due respect sir, the one out here in the bush with the most experience is usually in charge, and right now that is the Greek and me. In the air, you are in charge Lieutenant, but down here, experience trumps rank."

"Now you can order us to follow your instructions, and we will all probably end up dead. Do you want that on your shoulders LT?" Danny questioned.

For what seemed like an eternity, the pilot said nothing. In reality, it was probably only 15 seconds. He then looked up into Danny's eyes and said, "Marine, what do you suggest?"

"Well, sir, we are all up sh*t creek without a paddle, but I sug-gest we make two gurneys for Walker and the gunner and get out of here, pronto. And please take off those rank bars, those will get you killed!"

The pilot and co-pilot reached up and removed their bars. The pilot then asked, "Marine, what is your name?"
"They call me Dan Bo, sir, but it's Danny Lane. But, that is really not important. I am just a Marine trying to save our butts."

"How long have you been in the Nam?" The pilot asked.

"Less than 4 months sir."

"Are you a Sergeant?"

Danny laughs. "No sir, I'm only a PFC."

"Watching you throw down on Charlie from the helicopter tells me you have a lot of experience."

"Well sir, out here you either learn fast or you go home in a body bag. All of us have been together since day #1, and we're still alive." Danny pointed to the other Marines.

"That's the Greek, Combat, and Wells. We are Fire Team #1." He then points to the other Marines. "Those grimy a**es are Cohen, Tex, and Rootie Poot; Walker is the one hit. They are Fire Team #2. So, we better get our a**es moving — they will be all over us pretty soon."

"Combat, you and Wells go wire the chopper with C-4 enough to blow it sky high. We're not going to leave anything behind. Got it?" Danny ordered.

"Yeah, Dan Bo." Combat responded. "We got this." The pilots agreed, and the plan was made. Danny and the Greek would lead them all out of that h*ll hole.

The small band spent the next few minutes constructing two makeshift gurneys out of their ponchos for Walker and the dead gunner. Danny and the Greek lift ed Walker onto the gurney, then each took an end and boosted him into the air. Tex and Rootie Poot carried the gunner's body on the second gurney. They humped to a nearby safe area and waited for Combat and Wells to blow the chopper.

Combat and Wells waded across the chest-deep water and got into the half floating chopper. They finally got it wired and ran the detonation cord back onto the shore. They took cover behind some large elephant trees and blew the chopper into a million pieces.

"Th ere goes another million bucks of Uncle Sam's money." The Greek smirked as pieces of the once flying machine landed all around them.

"Well done," said the pilot, as Combat and Wells made their way to the group.

"I always wanted to blow up something really big." laughed Combat with pure delight.

"We've got to make tracks. I'm sure they are watching us right now, waiting for a place to kill all of us," Danny ordered.

"Dan Bo, I will take point," said the Greek.

"Sounds good. Combat, you take the rear. You know they will be following us, so be alert back there. Eyes and ears open men." Turning to the pilot, he said, "Sir, I want you and the co-pilot in the middle." They acknowledged him, and all the Marines started the slow, dangerous mission on the road to survival or death.

Crossing the jungle was slow going. The vegetation was as thick as the fog in the San Francisco Bay. The Greek took a machete and, slowly and deliberately, carved a path through the dense undergrowth. The solemn column weaved its way through the jungle like a caterpillar weaving its cocoon.

Hours passed and they had not encountered any resistance.

Combat continued to keep watch on the rear and flanks. He thought he saw movement off the left flank, and he signaled from the rear of the column. Danny halted the group and went back to talk to Combat.

"What you got?" Danny asked. "I think we have company man. I may be imagining it, but I swear I saw some bushes over there moving. You know how sneaky those little bast***s are." Combat said nervously. "I can feel them watching us Dan Bo."

"Yeah, I'm sure they are waiting for us to settle in for the night and then do us a job. Let's keep moving. Don't fire unless you have to; we don't know how many there are." Danny stated.

Danny motioned to The Greek to keep moving. The column moved out again, but this time more alert to their flanks.

However, one element completely out of their control was the growing darkness. The Greek held up his right fist, signaling the band to stop. He then whispered back to Danny, "Dan Bo, it is starting to get dark. I think we should stop for the night and start fresh in the morning."

"I agree," stated Danny as he looked around the jungle canopy for a place to set up camp.

"Alright, let's make camp here. The canopy is thick, and there are some good-sized trees. That will give us some cover."

They made the little camp as defensible as possible, then the Greek whispered to the band, "Ok, guys. Listen up. No talking, no eating, no mosquito repellent and no cigs.

Danny laughs. "No cigs?" I've never seen you go all night without a cig, Greek."

"Well, I will tonight my friend; duty calls."

Danny adds. "And no firing unless they are on top of us. We have limited ammo. Got it? Don't do anything except breathe!"

Danny motioned the group towards him with his hands and said, "Guys, gather around. Let's pray! We need the Almighty if we are going to get out of this. Lieutenant, what was the door gunner's name?"

"It was Cooper; Sergeant Chase Cooper. He was on his second tour. He had a wife and several kids back home. He was a good guy."

The band of tough, rugged Marines huddled together and took each other's hands. Danny bowed his head, and the others followed suit. Danny then prayed, "Heavenly Father, we need You. We feel isolated and we feel alone. We pray for Sergeant Cooper's family: please comfort his wife and kids; they don't even know that he is dead yet. How awful it will be when the Marines show up at their doorstep to give them the news. Please be with them. Lord, we also pray for Private First Class Walker, our brother who is wounded here in this jungle. Please heal his leg and help us to get him some medical assistance as soon as possible. And, God, we ask that You protect us and bring us through this night. In Jesus Christ's Name we pray, Amen."

As they lifted their heads, this small band had become brothers in a struggle for life or death. It sounds like a cliché, but in a deep dark jungle thousands of miles from where you safely read this book, it was deeply true.

As they got to their feet, Danny laid down some final instructions, "Combat, Wells, Rootie Poot, Cohen and Tex, I want you guys to make your way back up the trail and set up an ambush. Put trip flares all over the place. When they come, and we know they will, get your ass back here pronto. We will have a surprise waiting for them. Got it?" They all acknowledged.

The Marines settled in for a long night, but this time they would use the darkest of the night to their advantage. The trap was set; all they could do now was wait for the guests to arrive.

Hours passed well into the night, and all was relative calm — too calm. The jungle was active as it always is; the symphony of wildlife never rested. Wells heard something that didn't sound like an animal moving in the undergrowth. He touched Combat's arm to get his attention. Combat signaled Rootie Poot, Tex and Cohen. All five were on high alert, with adrenaline pouring through their veins. Hopefully, the enemy would trip the flares.

They weren't disappointed. Shortly after that, several flares were tripped. The startled NVA started shooting in all directions, not knowing where the Marines were. The Marines fired a volley of bullets into the enemy patrol and took off in a full sprint down the trail toward the other Marines.

Meanwhile, up the trail, Danny, the Greek, and the two pilots seen the flares go off, followed by the trumpet of bullets. "Here they come! Get ready!" yelled the Greek.

"Remember," said Danny. "Let our boys cross and light them up!"

As Wells and the others ran up the path, enemy bullets littered the dense jungle vegetation all around them. "Faster, boys. They are getting too close for comfort!" The enemy soldiers were closing in fast.

"You don't have to tell me to hurry up," said Rootie Poot as he ran past Wells like a track star in the Olympics.

As they finally crossed friendly lines, Danny, the Greek, and the two pilots lit up the enemy with all they had. Danny was using the monstrous M-60 machine gun that had been Sergeant Cooper's on the helicopter. Volley after volley went into the belly of the beast. After a couple of minutes, Danny held up a raised fist, signaling to the Marines to halt their assault.

All was quiet. The immediate danger was over.

"Don't move — stay put. You never know if they are dead, wounded or just playing possum. It will be daylight in a few hours. We will canvas the area then. Hold your positions and stay alert!" Danny ordered.

Morning came, and the Marines canvassed the area for dead bodies and intelligence. They discovered 12 dead bodies and no signs of wounded. The dead were NVA regulars fresh in the country, probably part of the NVA Divisions coming through Laos into South Vietnam from the Ho Chi Minh Trail that the Marines were trying to intercept.

The Marines broke camp and hiked all day through the dense jungle canopy. They finally reached a small clearing. The Lieutenant looked at his compass and said, "It looks like we are still about a day's hike away from Tomahawk. Division Headquarters knows our last coordinates — where we went down — and they know we would make our way towards Tomahawk. They won't stop searching for us. I suggest we stay here, at least for a while. They can get a chopper in that clearing."

"I agree," said Danny. "If we see a flyover, we pop the smoke, and hopefully they will see it."

Several hours went by. The Greek looked at his watch and nudged Danny. "What do you think, Dan Bo? It is getting late in the day again. You and I both know we won't all survive another night out here. We're about out of ammo."

The Marines were losing hope for a rescue when they heard the familiar sound of helicopters. Thank God America owned the skies over Southeast Asia. It was not only the rescue helicopter, but also two other battle choppers — the dreaded Huey Gunships.

Danny popped the red smoke grenade signaling their location, and the rescue helicopter slowly descended into the clearing. The Huey Gunships hovered up top, ready to take out any hostile and stupid move the enemy might be planning.

The Marines carefully loaded the body of Sergeant Cooper on board, and then the injured Walker. As the Marines lifted off the ground, their weary eyes met each other, but nothing was said. Nothing needed to be said. A respect had been born between these brothers that would never be broken. The Lieutenant looked at Danny and simply nodded. Danny nodded back. That was all . . . and that was enough.

CHAPTER SIX

FIREBASE TOMAHAWK: THE NOOSE TIGHTENS AROUND AREA BASE 112

IN THE LATE AFTERNOON ON FEBRUARY 14, 1969, Danny and his band of brothers had finally made it to Firebase Tomahawk. The rescue helicopter took the two pilots and the wounded and dead Marine on to Da Nang. Danny and the Marines were just in time for bunker watch. So much for some R&R after the chopper crash and the daring jungle escape from the clutches of the NVA.

Firebase Tomahawk sat on one side of the enemy's Area Base 112, while Firebase Maxwell sat on the other side. The Americans had conveniently surrounded the enemy like a lion stalking a gazelle. The noose had tightened, and it was time to take the enemy out.

The problem was, the enemy didn't want to go, and they had loaded Area Base 112 with some of their most experienced fighters. For the next two weeks, the Marines experienced the enemy's resolve. Patrols consistently found heavy resistance around the enemy base, and both American Firebases experienced mortar attacks and sapper assaults. It was true that the Americans repelled these attacks, but it was just a foreshadowing of what was to come.

On February 28, 1969, night came at its usual time. Danny was on bunker watch in their sand bagged fortress. Something seemed different about tonight. Was it the delirium caused by the malaria he had contracted, or was it something else? It was quiet — too quiet. Have you ever experienced something like that? On the surface, everything seems fine. But under the surface, you just know it is like a duck's feet below the water's crest. There is movement; lots of movement. You can't see it, but you can feel it in your bones. That is what Danny was experiencing on that given night.

Earlier, Danny and Fire Team #1 had set up trip flares and claymores in front of their foxhole. Claymore mines are valuable weapons for the Marines. A claymore mine is a directional fragmentation mine, with 700 steel spheres and 1-1/2 pound layer of composition C-4 explosives. It can kill anything within 50 yards of the explosion. It was a golden rule that the Marines would set out the claymores close to their location every night just before dark. They would collect them back every morning if not activated. The enemy was notoriously known for finding them and turning them around so the explosion would kill Marines. It was important to disguise them in the bush so they couldn't be found by Charlie.

Fire Team #2 with Cohen, Tex, Rootie Poot, and a new Marine, Daniel Bruce, who had joined the company a month earlier, were about twenty yards to the right of Fire Team #1. On the left was Fire Team #3 with Baker, Chicago, Calvin, and another new boot named Lewis.

Danny looked out into the darkness. He saw nothing. Everything seemed normal . . . as normal as it could be in Vietnam in the late 1960's. Danny closed his eyes to rest, but all his senses were on high alert. He listened intently, but heard only silence. Why was it so quiet? Where were the regular jungle sounds? They were muffled tonight. Was something in their midst that haunted them?

As he sat there in the darkness, surrounded by his buddies, the loneliness of his thoughts crept in. He thought about his grandmother, Nola; she had raised him. A smile creased the corners of his mouth as a memory flooded in. He was only four years old, and he was playing with green plastic army figures in a sandbox with his uncle, Larry. Larry was seven years old, and was like Danny's big brother.

"Grandma, I am going to be a soldier one day," said little Danny as he held two of his plastic green army men.

"I am sure you will, Sweetheart," said Nola. "Now, you need to quit chewing the heads off those little green men. When those are gone, they are gone. I am not going to buy you more if you keep chewing on them."

"I am sorry, Grandma. I won't do it anymore. But I really am going to be a soldier someday."

"And you will be a great soldier," said Nola, with a loving smile towards her grandson.

Danny then thought about the little Baptist church Nola had taken him and Larry to regularly. Another memory flooded to the surface. This time he was six years old, standing in a shallow creek near the church. Standing beside him was the minister. Danny remembered the fulfilled look on his grandma's face as she stood on the shore and watched her grandson give his life to Jesus Christ as his Lord and Savior and be baptized into Him.

All grown up now, and in a foxhole in Southeast Asia, a few drops of tears graced the corners of Danny's eyes. He was living his childhood dream. He was a soldier. As a small child, he hadn't understood the sacrifice that dream meant. He understood it all too well now.

With emotions raw and fear all too well, Danny prayed, "Oh, God, You know that I am far from home and about to enter into battle again with the enemy. I want to live, but Your will be done. My life is yours. I know I haven't always lived the way You have wanted me to, and I am a sinner just like everyone else. I thank You for being my Savior and freeing me from my sins. I pray now for my brothers in these foxholes with me. I pray for their Salvation. I pray that they know You, and I pray for our protection.

"Lord, I am wondering if this is my night to die. Why am I still alive, yet so many other soldiers have died? You must have a plan for me. Or does that plan end tonight? God, I am tired of worrying about death. I am exhausted and weary, and I feel like I am about to give up. Please give me Your strength and protection to endure this hell on earth. Lord, I need to hear You. Sometimes, all I can hear is the jungle. I need to hear Your message. Please give me peace. In the past, You have given me the strength to stand up for people who can't stand up for themselves. I ask for that strength tonight. Live or die; I am going to fight for what is right. God, I need You. In Jesus Christ's Name I pray, Amen."

For the next few moments, Danny listened intently for God. God did not speak in an audible voice, but He did speak to Danny in that quiet voice that encompasses your entire being. Danny felt a calmness and peace with whatever might happen. His fear was gone, and he knew that God was with him and that he could do what the Scriptures say: "For I can do everything with the help of Christ who gives me the strength I need." Philippians 4:13 (NLT)

Shortly after midnight, the silence was shattered by the disconcerting sound of *poouf, poouf, poouup*. Enemy tubes had launched their deadly arsenals. Soon, enemy mortars were raining down on the Americans. From the time you heard the tubes, to the time the explosion erupted was a matter of seconds. Not much time to take cover, and no time to prepare yourself.

"Incoming!" yelled Danny. The Greek, Combat, and Wells, who had been sleeping restlessly on the ground on the edge of the foxhole, all rolled into the hole as quickly as possible. Explosions rocked the entire American compound.

In the next moment, Danny's stomach sank, and it wasn't malaria this time. Enemy sappers burst through the jungle canopy blowing whistles and yelling "Chết, Joe" ... "Die, Joe!" Dressed in tan and khaki, their AK-47s launched a swarm of bullets towards Danny and his fellow Marines. Around their bodies, the sappers wore explosives — they were on a suicide mission. The sappers threw a satchel full of explosives into the American ammo dump storage. A chain reaction started almost immediately. Marines dove for cover, shrapnel soaring everywhere.

Combat and Wells both went down, hot shrapnel tearing into their soft flesh. The Greek and Danny had no time to attend to them now. The second wave of enemy sappers had burst into the clearing. Danny activated the claymores, and a wave of the enemy fell dead, but they just kept coming. There were so many of them. The Marines had entered the gates of Hades, and there appeared to be no way back out!

Danny lit into the enemy with his huge M-60 machine gun. The gun poured more than 500 rounds a minute into the invading monsters. The barrel was red hot with destruction. The Greek emptied 30-round clips one after another into the belly of the beast, but the beast continued to come.

"Broken Arrow!! Broken Arrow!!" Danny screamed. "Broken Arrow" is the code for being overrun. When a "Broken Arrow" is instituted, the rule is to shoot at everything that moves while staying put and staying down. In a nutshell, it means: hold your ground!

Training didn't prepare Danny for this kind of fighting. How could it? There was no simulation that could mimic this hell! As the enemy charged the Americans, an NVA sapper hurtled over a sandbag and invaded Danny's foxhole, landing on top of him. As Danny wrestled with the beast, he stretched to reach his Ka-Bar survival knife. His fingers grasped it, but then he was knocked off balance. Danny stretched again and got it. He immediately jammed the blade into the chest of the enemy. He rolled the sapper off of him and twisted the blade in deeper, finishing the beast once and for all.

"You alright, Dan Bo?" asked a concerned Greek.

Out of breath and nauseous, Danny responded, "Yeah . . . I'm Okay . . . How about Wells and Combat?"

"They will be okay. Just shrapnel; hit no arteries. They'll live."

For a few seconds, Danny squatted over the man he had just killed. He was a man, not a beast. Danny felt like he was going to vomit. To shoot a man from a distance was one thing; to stab him with a knife was totally different. It felt inhuman to Danny, as if *he* were the beast. This was a feeling that Danny would never forget. No war is glorious. No battle is sought after. The true warrior seeks peace and fights when all else fails. But there was no time to think of the moral ramifications — at least not now — because the enemy kept coming.

Danny and the Greek held their ground. The Greek glanced over at the bleeding Wells and Combat. He knew they needed to get them help as soon as possible. The ground around their foxhole was littered with dead Charlies. There were so many. Where were they all coming from? It was as if they had awakened a sleeping hornets' nest . . . and the hornets weren't too happy.

Fire Teams #2 and #3 had been hit hard. Danny heard a Marine yelling from the bunker on the right — It was Rootie Poot. "MEDIC UP! We need a corpsman, NOW!"

Danny grabbed an M-16 rifle off the ground in their foxhole. He curled some extra ammo around his forearm and said to the Greek, "Fire Team #2 needs help. I'm heading over."

"Go get em, Dan Bo. And be careful," said the Greek.

Danny found Cohen, Tex, and Rootie Poot carrying PFC Bruce back to the foxhole. Bruce appeared hit bad. As he reached the edge of their foxhole and climbed in, Danny asked, "What happened?"

"A sapper was about ten yards in front of us and threw a satchel charge," said Cohen. "Bruce snatched it out of the air like a wide receiver and ran with it."

"He saved our lives," said Rootie Poot.

"He is dead," said Tex. The Marines hung their heads for a moment; but for just a moment. In battle, there is no time to grieve.

Danny looked at his friends and said, "We are at Broken Arrow. We are overrun. Stay low and alert. Shoot at anything that moves!" Danny then slithered on his belly back to his own foxhole, to the Greek and the wounded Wells and Combat.

Explosions rocked the compound from the east to the west and the north to the south. Silhouettes of sappers could be seen running throughout the compound. Marines were picking them off one by one.

Just then, a high-pitched squeal was heard overhead. An enemy Rocket Propelled Grenade (RPG) was incoming. It was as if it sought out Danny. Danny instinctively lifted his head from his prone position. He saw nothing, but he knew the RPG was headed right for him. He just . . . knew. He scrambled to his feet and dove over a sandbagged mortar pit. As he did, the RPG exploded inches from the edge of the pit. The sandbags surrounding the pit burst apart, but Danny was alive, lying face-down in the pit with his hands over his head! How he was still alive, he did not know.

Danny was shaken from the blast, but he didn't appear permanently damaged. He then felt something wet coming from his ears, and noticed his hearing was muffled, as if he was wearing noise-canceling headphones. He touched one of his ears with his hand, and his fingers came away bloody. His ears were bleeding. What did that mean? Did his eardrums explode along with the RPG? Would his hearing become clear again? Even so, the enemy kept coming.

Danny glanced around. His mind was hazy. Did he have a concussion? The enemy was all around him. Danny wondered to himself, "Who is in charge of the compound now? Do we still have it, or does Charlie have it now? What is going to happen when we run out of ammo? Is this the end?" Danny sought answers, but came up with none. Then an awful thought glazed the corners of his consciousness: "At best, I am going to be a POW. I think I would rather die."

In the distance, a low roar could be heard. Could it be? Finally, some good news was on the horizon. *Spooky*, also known as *Puff the Magic Dragon*, was on his way. A small wave of relief fell on Danny's heart.

The American aircraft carried three 7.62 mm mini-guns that could fire 100 rounds per second. Imagine that! The mighty gunship could totally devastate a football-field-sized target in less than 15 seconds. And as long as its ammunition held out, it could re-engage in this destruction continuously, loitering over the target for hours. Danny and the Marines could use this type of loitering just about now.

Marines quickly marked the outer perimeter of the American lines with red flares. The kill zone was identified. Now it was time for Puff to do its magic. "Fire, Puff, fire," yelled the radio operator into the radio. "Repeat! Fire, Puff, fire! Kill zone is yours!"

Danny and all the Marines immediately put their heads down and tried to sink as low as they could into the moist foreign soil. Danny said a silent prayer to God that Puff was accurate. It is certainly a desperate move to have friendly fire called down upon yourself. But, this was a desperate time and required nothing less than a desperate move. Survival depended upon it.

All of a sudden, the air, ground, and life itself erupted with the mighty power of Puff. Bullets penetrated the ground just yards from the Marines like the sound of a summer downpour on a cool tin roof.

And as quickly as it began, it was over. An eerie quiet engulfed the compound. The air was thick with the smell of gunpowder, explosives, and death. Ever so slowly, Danny and the Marines began to push themselves off the ground to stand on their weary, shaky legs.

Then the search for their wounded comrades and any remaining intruders who survived Puff's assault began. Danny glanced up and saw Puff in the distance, circling the American compound 3,000 feet up like a protective hawk ready to pounce on any enemy movement on the ground far below. This necessary cover of protection allowed the medivac helicopters to land. One by one, the wounded and dead Americans were loaded onto the waiting helicopters.

Danny and the Greek helped load Combat, Wells and the hero Daniel Bruce onto a helicopter. "It looks like you guys are going to get that R&R you were looking for after all. And you didn't have to blow your own asses up," laughed Danny. "Charlie did it for you."

"You have a good trip over there to Japan, and get yourselves patched up," said the Greek.

Wells and Combat smiled at them and gave them a thumbs up. Danny and the Greek watched as the helicopter and their brothers flew away.

For the most part, Danny and the Greek came through the hellish night with only minor injuries. Danny's ears were still bleeding, and he had a migraine, but he felt blessed to be alive. Everything else seemed to be in good working order. The corpsman had wanted to put Danny on the helicopter with Wells and Combat, but Danny refused a trip out of this hell and a Purple Heart to stay with the Greek and get back at the enemy at Area Base 112. For his sacrificial heroism, Private First Class Daniel Bruce received the Congressional Medal of Honor.

Now that our troops were getting the care they needed, the job came to examine the dead enemy bodies that littered the entire compound like ants that had been sprayed with insecticide. Not surprisingly, Danny found packets of heroin and opium on the dead bodies of some of the NVA soldiers. It seems so odd to our military practices and values, but this was the norm for our enemy in Southeast Asia. The dead NVA soldiers appeared to be fresh troops from North Vietnam. Probably some of the same troops Danny had viewed on one of his many recon missions and killed after the helicopter crash. Their uniforms and equipment were obviously new, supplied graciously by the Chinese and the Soviets. This war kept on getting more complicated and difficult all the time.

The dead enemy bodies were quickly gathered up and stacked unceremoniously. No time to bury them now. Danny and his comrades had to prepare for the next wave of attacks, which were sure to come soon. This was, unfortunately, just the beginning of this nightmare for Danny and the Marines. They were now facing full and complete North Vietnamese Army Battalions. The Marines were undoubtedly outmanned. Danny just hoped that the Americans' advantage when it came to firepower would be enough. It had to be! It just had to be — or at least he hoped.

The Marines were in a desperate situation. They were running low on ammunition, food, and men. It was more than a mourning process for the dead; the Marines needed to logistically replace the men who had fallen.

The commanding officer called in air strikes to hit the suspected locations for Charlie, but the result was less than adequate. It could have been that Charlie had retreated underground. If that was true, the only way to get them out was for the Marines to go in on foot and pull them out of their dark caves like a fox snatching a rabbit from its hole. The Marines didn't have the manpower for that, so that option was a no go. It was better to hunker down until reinforcements arrived.

That was another thing: Regiment said that it could be days before the cavalry arrived. The Marines were told that the rest of 3/5 Company would be coming to help out, but that order was rescinded when the enemy hit An Hoa hard. Danny, the Greek, and their little band of Marines were on their own.

As for the much-needed supplies? When the CH-46 helicopters arrived, they were met with heavy enemy mortar fire which prevented them from landing. Danny and the Greek looked up into the bright sunlight and watched as their food and ammunition flew away, like a bird who has found the cat sitting on its nest. This day just kept getting better.

Danny, the Greek, and the Marines then went on to the only business at hand, which was to prepare for another night of death and destruction. They had to work quickly, because the night eternally trekked towards the Americans.

They reinforced their lines with as many sandbags as could be found, then stretched barbed wire around their foxholes. The CO then gave them an order that put a pit in their stomachs. "Marines," said the commander. "As you know, we don't have much ammo. We can't go around wasting it. Tonight, you must maintain fire discipline. It is a cliché, but 'don't shoot until you see the whites of their eyes.' You got that? Alright, let's get it done. We are holding this ground!"

Not long after that, Danny was sitting in his foxhole along with the Greek. With Combat and Wells on their way to Japan, their foxhole looked very empty. More importantly, with two men down, it was under-gunned. Dusk was falling. A few minutes passed, and the darkness came — the dreaded time had arrived. All the Marines were on high alert and poised for the inevitable.

"Well, here we go again, Dan Bo," said the Greek. "We have come a long way since boot camp. My friend, those commie bas**ards aren't killing us! You hear me? We are going to do the killing tonight!"

"You got that right, brother."

The Greek then took out his Greek flag and planted into the soil next to their foxhole. "Now those gooks will know who they are messing with!"

"A Greek and a Hillbilly — we can't lose," Danny said with a smile.

In total silence, Danny and the Greek sat there for what seemed like hours in the pitch black. A small rustle of sound came from the tree line that rattled their nerves. Was it Charlie coming to kill them? Or was it an animal? What goes through a soldier's mind when he is waiting for death to arrive? Well, that question has a million different answers for every soldier. For many, like Danny, you make peace with your thoughts and with death. If it was your time to journey to Heaven, then so be it.

If it was to be, then Danny wanted to die happy, and not 10,000 miles from home. So, he turned his thoughts homeward, to his grandmother, who raised him. She loved him more than life itself. The thought of her unconditional love put a small smile on the corners of Danny's mouth. For an instant, he wasn't in a dark, damp foxhole in Vietnam; he was in his grandmother's kitchen eating a hearty breakfast, without a care in the world. Danny then thought of the fun times in high school playing sports, and hearing his friends cheer his name. He also thought of the relaxing times hanging out with friends, and his music. Oh, how he loved his music. He could almost feel the rhythm in his mind as he and his band beat out a rock song at a gig. He would give anything to be behind his drum set at that moment, twirling his drum sticks through his fingers. But he wasn't. He was in a foxhole in Southeast Asia, waiting for the enemy's inevitable arrival. Oh, where was the dawn? Unfortunately, the night was young and the dawn was an eternity away.

Danny was shaken from his reverie as explosions began to rock the silence of the night. The enemy pushed through the brush, and the battle was on. It was fierce, but Danny and the Marines held their ground, then pushed back with a counterassault.

Letting his aggression out on the enemy, the Greek lifted himself halfway out of the foxhole and continued to pelt the enemy with his own fire of bullets. "Is that all you got, you commie bas**rds?"

As the words echoed from his mouth, he went limp and fell backward into the foxhole.

"Greek!!" yelled Danny. Was the Greek dead? Was his best friend gone from this earth? At that point, Danny couldn't check on his friend because of the barrage from the enemy. Danny hefted up his huge M-60 machine gun and began to devastate everything in front of their foxhole.

After a minute, which seemed like an hour, Danny ceased his fire and knelt by his friend. "Corpsman up . . . I need the Corpsman now . . . Corpsman up!"

With a weak smile, the Greek looked up at Danny, "I will be ok, Dan Bo. Just a slug in my shoulder. You get back at 'em for me, will you? Kick their butts!"

The Corpsman finally reached their foxhole. "What do we have, Danny?"

"The Greek has been hit in the shoulder. Quite a bit of blood."

The Corpsman immediately went to work on stabilizing the Greek. After a few minutes, he said to the Greek and Danny, "He'll live. He is too ornery to kill." The Corpsman then looked straight at the Greek and said, "We will get you out of here as soon as we can. You are going to get a little vacation at the hospital in Da Nang."

"Thanks, man," said the Greek.

As the battle raged on around them, Danny clasped hands with the Greek, then picked up the M-60 and began firing again. After a while, the pressure was too much for the enemy, and he retreated back into the bush. The Marines couldn't say that they had won round one — it was more accurate to say that they had survived round one. What concerned them was: would there be a round two that night?

After a night of sleeplessness, the dawn finally came. The Marines slowly began climbing out of their holes. They needed to get the wounded, including the Greek, out of the combat zone. It wasn't long before they heard helicopters approaching FSB Tomahawk. However, it wasn't the usual sound of the CH-46 Marine Chopper. With nerves on high alert and a lack of sleep, the first instinct was that the enemy was coming. But the enemy really didn't travel that way. Then the Marines realized what it was: it was the Army. The Cavalry was on its way. The helicopters were CH-47 Army Chinook Choppers, loaded with the much-needed supplies. These same helicopters would also Medivac the Greek and the other wounded to get the care they needed. Danny had never been so glad to see the Army. Forget the friendly rivalry between military corps; these were their brothers in arms, and they were coming to help.

The enemy continued to put pressure on the Americans daily. Danny had lost all of his Fire Team #1 members to combat wounds. He was alone for the first time without the Greek. Even though he was glad he was alive, and in a better place for now, he felt an emptiness like part of his soul was missing. He teamed up with members of Fire Team #2 and #3 and carried on as Marines do.

Danny and the Marines at Firebase Tomahawk fought every day and night. They had their supplies, but they were still on their own. The North Vietnamese Army had kicked their attacks into high gear against the Americans at An Hoa and Liberty Bridge, so all the other Battalions of the 5th Regiment were ordered to fall back in order to protect these key strategic locations.

Meanwhile, Firebase Maxwell had their own troubles nearby. Lima and Hotel Companies, and part of the H&S Company were on hand to help protect the firebase but, even so, the enemy was pushing inward towards them.

A Battalion of Viet Cong surrounded Lima Company, and they were pressured on all sides and all angles. Kilo Company got on the move to help their brothers in Lima Company, but were hit hard en route and were forced to pull back. So, Lima Company pushed forward alone and made heavy contact with the enemy.

Seventy-five enemy soldiers fell dead under the American defense. The Americans also took out two .50-caliber anti-aircraft positions, to the joy of our pilots.

For the next several days, Firebase Tomahawk continued to undergo enemy harassment. Danny and the troops waited with bated breath for Regiment to finally come up with an extraction plan.

On March 3rd, a Marine patrol was ambushed near Firebase Maxwell and three more Marines lost their lives. As the rest of the patrol was withdrawing, they tried to take the bodies with them. Americans don't leave a man behind, even in death. Unfortunately, the assault was so violent that they could only recover one of their fallen comrades.

The next day, the Marines returned and were able to recover one of the other bodies. The following day, they attempted to recover the third when they were ambushed again. Two more Marines were killed, and their bodies also had to be left behind. The situation kept getting worse. A couple of days later, the Marines again attempted to recover the bodies, when they were forced back by heavy enemy fire. When it was all said and done, the fallen American heroes were recovered by a reconnaissance team. Again, we don't leave a man behind.

On March 5, 1969, extraction plans were on the move to close both Firebases Maxwell and Tomahawk. The troops were needed back at An Hoa, which was experiencing heavy attacks. The Marines were able to close Firebase Tomahawk on March 5, and Firebase Maxwell closed on March 7.

Danny and the Marines had survived the gates of Hades in order to fight another day. It had been a long three months of combat. The North Vietnamese Army had been relentless. There was a fifteen-day stretch where attacks came day and night. The Marines had been outmanned by the swarm of enemy troops, but held their ground and their resolve. Now it was over. Time to move on to the next operation.

As the choppers lifted off under sporadic fire from the still-relentless enemy, Danny took a chance to glance out the small portal hole in the helicopter's side. He exhaled a puff of air in relief. He was alive, when so many others were dead. A flood of memories from the last 93 days flashed through his mind — the same memories that would haunt him on an almost nightly basis for the next forty years.

Danny's attention came back to the here and now, as movement below caught his eyes from the tiny window. Enemy soldiers were running up on Firebase Maxwell, shooting at the choppers as they ran. "Three months," thought Danny. "And we gave it back to them. What are we doing here? We fight! Many die. And for what? To give them the land we fought so hard to hold?"

From Command's point of view, the operation was a success. The Americans had successfully neutralized the enemy's Base Area 112. The Americans had captured 206 tons of rice, 430,000 rounds of ammunition, and 1,100 enemy weapons. Enemy losses were reported as 841 killed and another 182 soldiers captured. So, in many ways, the operation was a success. The flip side is told in what we lost that could never be replaced. *One hundred and eighty-three* Marines were killed in the operation, and another 1,487 were wounded. Lives were forever changed on those mountaintops on the other side of the world, known simply as Firebases Javelin, Tomahawk, Maxwell and Base Area 112.

CHAPTER SEVEN

CHARLIE BASE CAMP: A NOISY NEIGHBORHOOD

"SEE, HERE IS A PICTURE OF YOU WITH CHUCK Norris and Jean Claude Van Damme, working out. I think it was around 1982," said Chris to his dad as he sat at Danny's bedside in St. Mary's hospital. Danny was sitting up with a pillow behind his head and shoulders. Danny looked at the picture, but nothing seemed to register.

At that moment, Dr. McComas walked into the room. "Good afternoon, Chris."

"Good afternoon, Doctor."

"Well, I performed a spinal tap to remove a sample of the cerebrospinal fluid so that I could test it for infectious diseases, as well as any viral infections." The doctor paused, glanced down at his clipboard, and finally continued, "I discovered that your dad is suffering from a case of encephalopathy of an unspecified origin."

"What does that mean?" asked Chris.

"Well, basically it is a brain disease, or damage to the brain, that is causing a malfunction. It can be caused by a viral infection that creates a swelling of the brain. I think that is what is going on here. Encephalopathy can cause a broad spectrum of symptoms, which can express themselves in the forms of memory loss, dementia, seizures, coma . . . even death in some cases."

With that, Chis' cheeks turned white as a ghost. Dr. McComas realized that the news had stressed the young man, but he believed in being a straight shooter with as much compassion as possible. "The problem is that there are hundreds of such brain diseases and at this point, I can't pinpoint which one your dad is suffering from. I am sorry, Chris."

Dr. McComas took a deep breath and exhaled it slowly before continuing. "I am researching some studies that were performed on combat veterans from the Vietnam War, to see if we can begin to narrow down any specific brain ailments. Your dad was exposed to all kinds of chemicals and pathogens during his military tours. He was exposed to many jungle viruses, including malaria, which we know for a fact he contracted. He could have ingested parasites from contaminated water — and he was even exposed to Agent Orange. What we know at this moment is that his brain is very swollen, and we have to address that immediately. He is in a very critical state right now. If we can't get this under control . . . then we could lose him.

"I need to bring up another topic too," said Dr. McComas. "We need to appoint someone to be your father's Power of Attorney in order to authorize future decisions concerning his health and other affairs."

"I'm the only one he has, Doctor. I will call some of his lawyer friends and get it done."

"Good. I am sorry I don't have better news for you at this point. Hopefully we will have some good news soon," said Dr. McComas. "If he doesn't respond to treatment then we may have to move him to a Veterans Hospital or a nursing home. At this point, he needs twenty-four-hour care. Unfortunately, our hands are a little tied because he has no insurance outside the Veterans Health Administration."

With that, the doctor slowly and solemnly walked from the room. Chris was left with only his own thoughts to process, along with the vacuum of a man staring intently at him.

THE HELICOPTER hovered over the landing at An Hoa on March 5, 1969, and Operation Taylor Common was over. As it did, the wind created by the rotor blades kicked up sand and dirt. Danny could feel the thud as the chopper made contact with the ground. It wasn't home, but at least it was the rear area — if there was such an area in Vietnam.

Danny stepped off the CH-46 and realized how tired he was. The adrenaline was gone, and energy seemed to seep from every corner of his body. As he walked, he scratched an itch on his unshaven face. He was hungry, exhausted, and very much in need of a shower. After all, it had been 93 days since he had last washed himself. Can you imagine that? Most Americans can't go a day without a shower. Try 93 days!

Danny and the other Marines slowly made their way through the massive compound, towards the tents. The hell on earth they had experienced for the last three months showed on their faces. They were hardened, callused, and even a bit numb to certain emotions. They had experienced too much, especially for those so young.

Danny walked into his tent and dropped his equipment next to his bunk. He then sat on the bunk and reached down to take off his mud-caked boots. As he did, he noticed numerous empty racks (bunks) around him. The Greek, Combat, and Wells were not there. All were alive, and Danny took solace in that, but he certainly felt their absence. As he looked at the other empty racks, his mind went to the faces of his comrades in Fire Teams # 2 and # 3 who would never be seen again. Many had paid the ultimate sacrifice.

He paused with his hands still holding his laces and thought to himself, "So many dead!" He hadn't been close to them, but all the same, they were brothers, and now they were gone. Danny reached back down, took off his boots, and began to change his clothes.

As Danny grabbed some fresh clothes, he looked at his bare-skinned, emaciated body. He had lost a lot of weight. There were many causes. Of course, the stress of being on edge for three months would take its toll on anyone. Top this off with the almost unbearable heat and malaria and the pounds fell off his body like a heavyweight boxer trying to cut weight before a title fight.

Danny's head was bothering him a lot. He was suffering daily from severe migraine headaches, caused partially by the concussion he received when that RPG explosive almost took his life.

Danny went to the shower, which was actually a little outdoor hut, and scraped and scrubbed the layer after layer of grime, dried sweat, dirt, and blood off his skin. He had thought he had a pretty good tan going after being in the sun for so long, but after his shower his skin was as white as snow. All that wartime grime makes for good sun protection. But it still felt good to be clean.

Later that evening, a soldier came around with the mail. Mail time was always a happy time for the troops. Any word from the real world was a breath of the freshest air to the driest of lungs. The Greek had received a letter from his sweetheart, Sophia. Danny told the soldier he would take the letter for the Greek. As Danny held it in hands, he could smell the sweet perfume Sophia had put on the envelope.

Danny didn't have a love of his life. He wondered if he ever would. In fact, he didn't even have any mail. To tell the truth, he wasn't sure anyone even knew where he was or if he was still alive. However, he realized it was partly his fault, because he hadn't told anyone he was going to Vietnam.

As he sat there holding the Greek's letter, he made a decision. He would write his mother. He wasn't close to her. But she was his mother, and she deserved to know where he was and that he was alive.

Dear Judy,

Just a quick note to say I am ok and still alive. I wanted to give you my address here in Vietnam so maybe you could send me a care package full of my favorite snacks, and maybe some liquor for my squad.

You know I love Snyder Potato Chips and Fig Newtons more than anything, so it would be nice if you could do that.

I just got off an Operation that lasted 93 days. I have been very sick, and have lost a lot of weight from malaria and from a lack of food. I have been here for four months, and have been living in a foxhole in the jungle every day but two.

It is hard to describe what this war is like, and what I have had to do to stay alive. Death is all around me every day. I'm don't really know why we are here or what we are fighting for. None of the Vietnamese seem to want us here.

What is going on back in the States? We have no way of knowing; not much news available. We have no contact with the outside world. I even lose track of time. Most of the time I don't know what month it is, let alone the day of the week.

Most of our fighting is done at night. I hate the nights. Everything bad happens when it is dark out. So many Marines have died around me. Most of the time, I don't even know their names. My friend, Sotere, from Cleveland — we call him the Greek — got shot the other day. He is alive, though, and expected to live.

Well, I'd better go. I need to rest up and get ready for another assignment. We never know what is going on; we just follow orders.

You can mail the package to the address on the envelope. This is the regimental address.

If I am on an operation, it will be here when I get back. Please send extra potato chips.

Your son,
Danny

Danny and the other soldiers tried to relax for a while before nighttime came yet again. This night, though, was different. It was uneventful. The Marines needed such a night. They got some much-needed sleep, even though it was not restful. The American artillery and mortar batteries fired H&I's all night long. H&I stands for Harassment and Interdiction. The strategy was to fire at known and suspected enemy locations from which the enemy staged their attacks on An Hoa.

Danny received something he hadn't expected during his time at An Hoa — he got promoted. He was now a Lance Corporal and promoted to Fire Team Leader. Four months earlier, Danny had been sitting on a wet, cold tarmac as a boot ready to face his first mission, and now he was a leader of men. Well, a few men anyway.

Corporal Kessler told Danny that the Greek had been promoted too, and would be given his own Fire Team when he recovered. Danny was happy for his friend. He was also a little sad, because he wouldn't see his friend quite as much. At least they would still be in the same Squad and Platoon. What a change in four months. In wartime, four months is a lifetime. That is why, during a war, soldiers are promoted faster than they are in peacetime.

It may seem odd, but one of the most glorious luxuries in the rear area was being able to use a wooden latrine instead of the next leaf out in the bush. Danny happened to be sitting there doing his business when he heard the faint scream of the enemy 122mm rockets. He maintained his position because the rockets were obviously far in the distance. However, the whine began to get closer and closer. Danny sat there, wondering what to do. Meanwhile, the scream of the rockets got louder.

Danny tried to hurry, but that just made it worse. He then had to make a decision. With his pants around his knees, he jerked up and flung the wooden door almost off its hinges. He ran as fast as he could with his trousers hovering around his ankles and dove into the fortified bunker close by. He made it just as the toilet and its contents were blown to pieces by an enemy rocket. The other Marines in the bunker looked at the scared expression on Danny's face, then looked at his pants and burst into laughter.

Shortly after the toilet debacle, Danny's company heard that they were moving to nearby Charlie Base Camp, relieving another company. Charlie Base Camp was a very well-fortified location about a mile from An Hoa. It was on the road to Liberty Bridge. Once there, Danny and company would provide security for the Regimental Base at An Hoa until the next operation was to commence.

One of Danny and his Fire Team's responsibilities was to provide security on daily patrols to sweep the road for possible mines left overnight by the VC and NVA. Not a fun duty because of the obvious hazards, but nevertheless one that was extremely important in order to keep the road safe and open for military and local transportation. The minesweeping itself was done by the military engineers. The engineers would use electronics to locate any hidden mines, while the Marines walked behind them in order to provide security.

Directly across the dirt road from Charlie Base Camp, separated only by a barbed wire fence, was the tiny village of Duc Duc. The VC and NVA were known to infiltrate and blend in with the villagers so that they could launch their attacks with haste and secrecy. So the Marines swept the village and all the huts on a regular basis, looking for any signs of the enemy. The villagers just wanted to be left alone. They were trapped between the Americans and the North Vietnamese. The villagers lived in straw huts, had no running water, and ate rice most of the time. What change of life were they going to have if we brought freedom to their country? In fact, they didn't care. Freedom or no freedom, they just wanted to live without fear of dying every day.

Even though Charlie Base Camp was considered the rear area, it had its own challenges. It was surrounded by high mountains. The enemy sat up in those mountains and regularly launched rockets with pinpoint accuracy, raining destruction and fear down on the Marines.

As I mentioned a few moments ago, Charlie Base Camp was well fortified. It had large, sandbagged bunkers, hundreds and hundreds of feet of barbed wire, a command center, and trenches that were two feet underground. The Marines crawled through these trenches during enemy rocket attacks. The base also had a battery of 106mm recoilless rifles and 81mm mortars, as well as other weapons to counter the enemy attacks.

One of the greatest temptations for the Marines was to buy merchandise from the villagers at Duc Duc. They sold a rum that was made out of sugar cane, and a drug called ganja weed. Other drugs such as opium and heroin were also sold by the villagers.

The Marines were warned and ordered not to buy anything from the villagers. They couldn't be trusted, as many of them were VC in disguise. In the past, villagers had crushed small slivers of glass and placed them in the rum bottles. The crushed glass was so fine that you couldn't see it with the naked eye, but when swallowed it would tear at your throat and insides like cancer to the bones. A very painful, slow death.

One particular night, Danny and a few Marines had gathered around the 81mm mortar pit. As he walked up, Parker, a new boot in the mortar team, proudly displayed his trophy. With his right arm raised in the air and a bottle held firmly in his grasp, Parker exclaimed, "Hey, guys! Look what I got! I got me some of that homemade rum."

Parker wanted to share his purchase with his buddies. Almost immediately, Danny and some of the other Marines fervently protested, repeating the company line that the villagers couldn't be trusted. Parker sloughed it off with a smirk and a shake of the head, "Nay, it is alright. It was an old lady I bought it from. She had to be older than my grandma. Come on! Let's have some!"

With that, Parker opened the bottle, lowered his nose to the white liquid, and took a sniff. He then cocked his head back and took a large swig from the bottle. Instantly, Parker screamed in pain. He fell to the ground. By the time Danny reached him, blood was oozing from the corners of his mouth. Parker was dying, and there wasn't anything Danny could do to stop it. Danny yelled for the Corpsman. Parker was dying a slow, painful death — there was nothing the Corpsman could do either. Danny watched as the life seeped out of another Marine . . . and Charlie hadn't even fired a shot.

On deeper inspection of the bottle, it was discovered that it contained small slivers of glass, just like they had been warned. With anger, frustration, and anguish, Danny looked at the Marines and firmly said, "Don't trust any of those Gooks, you got that? Don't be stupid!"

Parker was a now going home in a body bag, with no explanation to his parents for his death. The Marine Corp wasn't about to tell them that their son had died from "being stupid." Parker's death would simply be listed as "unexplained," and would become part of the statistics for how soldiers died in Vietnam.

Danny was still suffering the effects of malaria and the rocket explosion that had bloodied his ears. He had lost so much weight that he appeared emaciated, and the migraine headaches had gotten worse. Danny barely functioned during the day. The sunlight seemed to bore a hole directly into his skull. The Corpsman gave him the painkiller Darvon, but it didn't even touch the pain.

The headaches got so bad that Danny had great difficulty sleeping. He began having a very vivid dream about his own death. In the dream, Danny saw a casket. He saw the mourners making their way up to the casket to pay their respects. There were his friends from high school. Then came the guys from his rock and roll band. Oh, and there was the sweet face of his grandmother, Nola, who had raised him, as her heart broke looking down on Danny.

Danny had been born Daniel Edward Jeffers. His mother, Judy, had given Nola custody of Danny at his birth. In all manner of speaking, Nola was really Danny's mother. Judy was more like an aunt. But Judy was Danny's biological mother, and he respected her simply because of that fact. At the time, Judy was married to Oscar Edward Jeffers, but Ed, as they called him, never saw Danny throughout his childhood.

After her marriage to Ed had ended, Judy married a good man named Oliver Lane in 1959. Oliver was a Marine and Army veteran. For four years, Danny lived with his mother and Oliver. Oliver adopted Danny, and that is how he became Danny Lane. This was the only time in his life where Danny felt like he had a traditional family.

In his dream, Danny looked down at himself in the casket. You can imagine how unnerving it was for him to look down upon his own dead face. He was lying perfectly still in his Marine dress blue uniform. He heard the eulogy so clearly it was as if someone was whispering into his ear with a megaphone. *"Danny Lane, a decorated Marine hero, died May 31st, 1969, in combat in Vietnam . . . He was only twenty years old. Danny Lane is preceded in death by his step-father, Oliver Lane. . ."*

Night after night, Danny would be awakened by a cold sweat and sheer terror. Night after night, it was the same dream. What did it mean? Was he really going to die? Was it a sign from God?

Danny went back to the Corpsman, who gave him some more meds which would hopefully take the pain away and let him sleep peacefully. Nothing worked. The dream kept coming. Eventually, Danny hated to go to sleep, even during the daytime. The dream would always come. He couldn't shake it or get away from it. Finally, Danny accepted it. If it was his time to die on May 31st, then it was his time. There was nothing he could do about it. He gave the situation to God and decided that he would die with honor.

By mid-April, the Greek had returned from Japan, where he had been recuperating from his wounds. He had also been promoted to Lance Corporal and was put in charge of Fire Team #2. Wells and Combat returned to the unit shortly after the Greek, and both got promoted to Lance Corporal too. While on rest & relaxation (R&R) in Australia, Combat had purchased a stuffed koala bear that said, "I love you, mommy" when you pulled its string. He gave it to the Greek as a gift. Even though he knew Combat was razzing him, the Greek couldn't help but love the stuffed animal. He carried it in his backpack from that day forward.

Danny, the Greek, Wells, and Combat found themselves surrounded by a lot of fresh faces. The Unit had several new boots in its ranks. Some of it was because of normal troop rotations, but unfortunately, much of it was from the loss of Marines.

Things had been fairly quiet at Charlie Base Camp. Well, quiet is a relative word. I should say quiet for Vietnam. The VC still attacked constantly, but their movements were more of the harassing variety. No massive attacks, just enough to keep Marines on edge.

Soon, that would all change. It was a muggy, night late in early May. It all started as usual. Danny was now in the command center, monitoring radio communications from the different company checkpoints. All was well.

The command center itself wasn't anything more than a well-fortified, sandbagged bunker where they kept the electronic equipment. If necessary, this bunker was where Danny would call in artillery strikes to take out suspected enemy attack positions. Danny was thinking about his Snyder Potato chips and Fig Newtons as he glanced over the radio controls. He had, that very day, received a care package from his mother. She had packed in it some of Danny's favorite snacks: Fig Newtons, potato chips, candy bars, and even some whiskey . . . Kentucky Bourbon. The whiskey was of the brown variety, and Danny hated brown liquor, but his mom didn't know that. He appreciated it anyway, and his squad definitely had their eyes on it.

Around midnight, the potato chips, Fig Newtons, and whiskey had to be forgotten. The sound of a mortar and rockets could be heard coming from the mountains above Charlie Base Camp. With seconds to respond, the Marines scrambled for cover.

Within moments, the compound lit up. Hot metal flew in all directions. Keeping his head down, Danny slithered on his belly to the radio to call in support. Was this a single enemy barrage they were experiencing, or the start of something more? No one knew . . . best not to take any chances.

After a few minutes, all was quiet. Too quiet. Danny walked out from his bunker and felt like he was looking into a fog. Smoke hovered low throughout the compound. The air also smelled of explosives. After a quick check, it was discovered that there were no serious casualties.

The deathly quiet soon ended, with the dreaded sound of enemy missiles coming again from the mountain top. The whine that filled the quiet told the Marines that a large enemy volley was raining down. Danny needed to call Regiment to try to get some of our own big guns to bombard the mountain. First, he had to pinpoint the enemy position as best he could in order to give Regiment accurate coordinates.

Then, the sound of small arms fire could be heard from 360 degrees around the compound. Charlie was coming! Danny looked at one of his fellow Marines and said, "Tex, go outside and see if you can pinpoint where the flashes are coming from." Observing the enemy flashes would give the Marines the location of the enemy launch sites.

Tex headed toward the entrance of the bunker. He hesitated just a bit at the entrance, then took another step. In hindsight, that was the last step he would take that night. Just as he exited the bunker, an enemy bullet seared towards him and into his left leg. Tex screamed in pain and fell back into the bunker.

Danny quickly made his way to Tex. Upon examination of the wound, Danny discovered that the bullet had entered and exited Tex's body. He was lucky. Danny said, "Tex, listen to me. You are going to be ok. The bullet came out. It was a through and through. You are going to be alright! You hear me? We will get a medic in here as soon as we can."

Now it was up to Danny. He had to pinpoint the location of the enemy rocket launchers, as well as get the Corpsman to help Tex. Danny eased his way out of the safety of the command bunker and into the chaos of flying bullets. The bullets were coming from the village across the dirt road. It sounded like the 30-caliber machine guns that the NVA used.

Bullets flew everywhere. It was like being buzzed by deadly bees. The enemy tracer bullets lit up the night sky like lightning bolts inside a tornado. Danny knew that for every tracer he saw, four more bullets were in between. For the moment, he dropped down into a trench that was several feet below the surface of the ground. He laid on his back and watched the light show unfold.

After a few minutes, the thought of those snacks in his tent returned to Danny's mind. It is funny what a soldier will think about during the firestorm of battle. Danny decided to crawl to his tent, which was nearby, and get himself some the potato chips and Fig Newtons out of his care package from home. It looked like it was going to be a long night . . .

Danny flung open the tent flap and crawled through the opening. He went over to his bunk, grabbed the Figs and potato chips, and thought to himself, "I am going to need something to wash this down." He then grabbed the liquor, and off he went with his stash.

He crawled back towards the command bunker, but got pinned down again by the intense fire coming from the village. Glancing upward, he saw that the night sky looked like the Fourth of July. There were explosions and tracer bullets everywhere he looked.

With nothing else to do, Danny ripped open the potato chips and rammed a handful into his mouth. A steak dinner wouldn't have tasted any better to Danny on this given night. Danny then shoved a couple of Fig Newtons into his mouth — after all, a soldier has to have dessert. By this point, Danny was pretty thirsty. He opened up the whiskey and took a swig. The 140-proof burned his throat all the way down into his belly, which was now content. Since there was no lull in the action, Danny kept up his little smorgasbord for a while and then scuttled to a nearby bunker that was facing the village.

Inside he found the Greek, Chicago, Rootie Poot, and Hillbilly locked and loaded, waiting to unload on the village if given the order. Surprisingly, they were singing "We Gotta Get Out of This Place" by the Animals. The song was playing on a large transistor radio Chicago got on R&R. Together they were all singing "We gotta' get out of this place, if it's the last thing we ever do . . . We gotta' get out of this place Cause girl, there's a better life for me and you."

Bullets were bouncing all around the fortified bunker as the Greek saw Danny crawling in with a half-full whiskey bottle and the remnants of snacks. Greek said, "Come on, man. What's with that, Dan Bo? You didn't save anything for us?"

"Hey, I was pinned down. I had to do something to pass the time," said Danny.

Chicago, who was a big African American from the Windy City, reached out and tried to grab the bottle from Danny. "Hey man, give me some of that, bro."

"No can do, Chicago," said Danny with a smile. "This is the good stuff."

With his gold-capped front teeth shining in the dim night light, Chicago said, "Why do you think I want it, bro? It is because it is the good stuff."

Danny then took a good sniff of the air around him and said, "You boys have been doing a little partying of your own, haven't you?" The smell of ganja weed was as thick as a girl's cheap perfume on a Saturday night in Oceanside . . . except it didn't smell as good.

"Hey, we have to pass the time too. Not going to let those gooks spoil our party. We got a fresh stash over at the village today. It is supposed to be some real primo stuff," said Rootie, as he offered Danny a hit from his freshly-rolled joint. Danny wrinkled his nose at Rootie's offer. "Get that stuff away from me, Rootie. You guys know I'm allergic to any kind of cigarette smoke."

"Too bad Dan Bo. Guess that makes more for us," laughed the Greek.

The festive mood inside the bunker suddenly shifted as the sounds of the battle outside intensified. Looking out, Danny could finally determine that the RPGs (rocket-propelled grenades) and machine gun fire were coming from inside the village. Several of the huts were on fire. An old lady in the midst of the firestorm was tossing buckets of water on her burning home.

The VC and NVA were notorious for putting the villagers in harm's way and using them as human shields. Many times the villagers were VC in disguise. Danny positioned himself behind Chicago's M-60 machine gun that was mounted on the sand bags strategically pointed at the village. He pinpointed the area that the enemy machine gun fire was coming from, carefully aimed at the threat and opened up with short bursts. Other villagers were screaming and running throughout the village. Enemy fire from the village intensifies. Danny opens up with the M-60 full automatic on the village. The old lady pouring water onto her hut suddenly goes down in the crossfire.

"Da** it! What the he** is she doing out there trying to put the fire out in the middle of a firefight?" Danny screams. He knew it was his bullet that had ended the old woman's life. He had no time to pray for forgiveness or second guess his decision. This night, and this exchange, would haunt Danny in his dreams for four decades.

Danny knew what he had to do next. He needed the authority from Regiment to call in artillery strikes to take out the once-friendly village. By doing so, Danny knew that innocent men, women, and even children would be killed. But what options were there? The Marines were being bombarded by enemy artillery in the mountains, as well as ground fire and RPGs from the village. Danny knew what was next if he didn't do anything; the enemy ground assault would be the next wave, and Danny feared being overrun again. The madness had to be stopped, and it had to be stopped now.

Danny left the safety of the bunker and his friends and crawled back toward the command center. The bullets soared overhead as thickly as fog. Once inside the command center, Danny briefed the CO. The CO called Regimental Headquarters in An Hoa. He got the order from Command to fire at will at Duc Duc. Danny wrote down the coordinates for the village —he had to be precise to avoid taking as many innocent lives as possible.

He got on the horn and called it in, "M10, this is Mike 1A, adjust fire, over."

"Mike 1A this is M10, adjust fire, over."

"Grid ES 923 945, over."

"Grid ES 923 945, over."

Danny continued, "Unknown number of enemy embedded in the village with 30-cals and RPGs. Civilians close by, friendlies close by, 'danger close,' send spotting rounds . . ."

"Roger, on the way!" said the Regiment radio officer.

Danny went outside to view the spotting rounds. The spotter rounds are non-explosive rockets used to pinpoint the exact coordinates without doing the destructive damage. Danny could hear the blast from the distant artillery battery. The spotters were on their way. As the spotters landed, the white phosphorous rounds known as "Willie Pete" caught the nearby huts on fire. Villagers scattered. They knew from experience what was to follow. Danny saw that the spotters were on target to take out the enemy. He ran back into the command center, grabbed the radio, and said, "Fire for effect, over . . ."

"Roger, fire for effect, out!" said the artillery unit radio officer.

Danny tossed down the radio and ran back outside to watch the incoming American missiles launched from An Hoa. Suddenly, the rockets could be heard as their high-pitched scream filled the air. A moment later the village lit up like a Christmas tree. Screams of a different sort were now heard from the village as silhouettes of villagers could be seen running in all directions. One villager ran as flames engulfed his body, and then he was down . . . forever. As he squinted through the night air and smoke, Danny could see village elders carrying dead bodies, maybe even the bodies of their family members. It was hard to watch, and it was hard to forget. War is tragic, and decision points can be difficult, but sometimes both are necessary.

The Medivac was able to extract Tex and, miracle upon miracles, no other Marines were wounded or killed that night. The fortified bunkers were a true blessing.

Finally, the terrible night ended as the sun poked its head above the horizon. A patrol was sent to the village. Smoke was still lingering in the air. The village itself was in ruins. Carnage was everywhere, both human and animal. Medics and transports were brought in to take the lucky villagers who were only wounded, instead of dead.

Danny and his squad found the 30-caliber machine guns and the dead VC soldiers that had been manning them. Other enemy weapons were also found, justifying the decision to take out the village. Later that day, bulldozers were brought in to clear the debris. The Marines also buried the dead villagers to show honor, respect, and sorrow for the unfortunate loss of life. Danny hated this place 10,000 miles from home. Would it ever end? Maybe all too soon. After all, Danny had his own potential date with destiny and death. This was one dream Danny hoped wouldn't come true.

The next several weeks were strained with the villagers to say the least. But the Marine's duties were as routine as routine can be in the Nam. Early morning you would do mine sweeps on the road to An Hoa and Liberty Bridge. Afternoons, you would go on security patrols in the village and the surrounding area, then try to get some afternoon shut-eye. Evening and nights were always bunker watch.

In late May 1969, Corporal Kessler was promoted to Sergeant and rotated back to the world. His tour was done and he was going back to the world in one piece. He was a great leader and led Danny and the young Marines through many battles. He would be missed by the First Squad. Danny was surprisingly promoted to Corporal and assigned to be the First Squad leader. He had moved up two ranks since he got there 7 months ago. He would now be leading all three Fire Teams into battle. It was a big responsibility, but it was one that he was willing to take.

The Greek was now the Fire Team #1 leader, Combat would lead Fire Team #2 and Wells would lead Fire Team #3.

Word just came down that a new operation was being launched soon. Time for Danny and his Marines to prepare for battle in the bush again.

CHAPTER EIGHT

OPERATION PIPESTONE CANYON: A DATE WITH DEATH

DANNY WOKE UP AND LOOKED AROUND THE dimly-lit room of St. Mary's hospital, unsure of when or where he was. The sunshine was just beginning to peek in the tinted window to his right. This was wrong. This was not his room. He broke into a sweat as a wave of panic began to wash over him. He glanced down to his left. Several wires hung from his arm, and pads were attached to his chest. Danny's mind raced as the fear grew. Was he a prisoner? Were the Viet Cong conducting insidious experiments on his body? Were they torturing him to get vital military information? "Name, Rank and Serial Number is all I will give them," thought Danny.

At that moment, the door to his opened, and a man walked into the room. He had a kind face and a gentle smile form-ing on the corners of his lips. Was this some sort of a trick to make him feel comfortable before they tortured him?

The man opened his mouth, and words spilled out: "Hi Mr. Lane! How are you today? I am Dr. McComas. Do you remember me?" Danny said nothing. "Well, that is ok. Even if you can't talk today, maybe you can hear and understand me."

"As you can see, we are in a different room today," continued Dr. McComas. "I have moved you out of the ICU and into a private room. You are receiving some strong antibiotics.

We are using the IV in your arm to administer the medication and hopefully reduce the swelling in your brain, as well as the viral infection. I have sent some of your brain fluid to the Mayo Clinic so that their specialists can analyze it."

"We have to continue to build up your strength, so you are receiving supplements full of nutrients. I see you have the notebook I asked your son Chris to bring to you. Let me write down my name on it. I will put it right beside your son's name. I am also writing down today's date, your name, and the location of where we are today. You are at St. Mary's Hospital in Huntington, WV. Mr. Lane . . . Danny, I am going to ask you questions about this information every time I come in to see you."

Dr. McComas walked over and turned on the television set. He flipped the channels until he found one of the 24-hour cable news channels. He handed Danny the remote control. "Here is the control. Switch it to any channel you want. But I would like you to watch some news today to catch up on what is going on in the world. Do you understand?"

"Yes, Sir!" Danny said in a soft but firm, unmistakably military tone. Dr. McComas was taken back by this response.

"Danny, somewhere along the way your brain checked out from reality and into a world all your own. I need to find out why and help you back, if I can." Dr. McComas gently tapped Danny's leg, which was covered with a thin sheet. "You hang in there." With that, Dr. McComas turned and walked towards the door. As he did, he heard a soft whisper over his shoulder.

"Thank you, Sir. "The doctor paused and turned back to his patient. "You are most welcome, Mr. Lane."

IT WAS 5 AM, May 26, 1969. The sun was not even beginning to poke up on the distant horizon. Danny lay on his backpack and looked up at the early morning sky. If it was anywhere else, it might have been a peaceful setting. But this was not peaceful, and this was not anywhere else. This was Vietnam, and Hades was on the move.

The ground shuddered under the pressure of heavy bombardment, bouncing Danny's body a few inches off his pack and then back down again. The Americans were pushing back against this hell. Operation Pipestone Canyon was commencing with a blistering bombardment of the Area of Operation for the Western region. The Naval ship the USS Newport News sat offshore and launched heavy, 8-inch (203mm) shells one after another. This area was going to be tamed . . . or obliterated in the process.

As Danny lay there watching the fireworks overhead, he wondered why they were ordered to go into enemy territory again in the dark. Everything was harder at night — not to mention more terrifying. Not being able to see or probe for booby traps with every step would be deadly for the Marines. "But," Danny thought, "we are Marines; we do what we are told, and we go where we are sent."

Danny and about a thousand other Marines from the 3rd Battalion 5th Marines were staged at Liberty Bridge near An Hoa. They were waiting for the massive bombardment overhead to cease so that they could get on the move. The bombings focused on "Dodge City" and the "Arizona Territory." Danny knew that the massive bombing was also intended to help activate the booby traps awaiting the unsuspecting Marines. Danny hoped the bombings would get all the traps, but he knew they wouldn't. Obviously, the Marines weren't going to have a quiet stealth approach.

Danny kept his thoughts to himself, but the frustration plagued his mind. "What was the point of all of this? Months earlier we kicked their butts in this territory during Operation Meade River." You see, the Marines were about to head back into the territory where they had been before. Vietnam was a frustrating war where they would take a hill, only to allow the enemy to have the hill back again.

This contiguous area of Dodge City and Go Noi Island was ten to twenty kilometers south of Da Nang, and not more than twenty kilometers west of An Hoa. There was also a north-south railroad berm that bisected the area. This relatively small piece of land was to become a crucial point in many battles to come for Danny and his company. Danny's prophetic date with death in five days was becoming closer and more likely.

The land itself was mainly flat, but was covered with many obstacles, including rice paddies, extremely thick brush, hedgerows that were tangled knots, and vast expanses of elephant grass. However, the greatest obstacle for the Marines was the villages. There were nearly two dozen villages along their route, and they were infested with the Viet Cong disguised as villagers who just wanted to be left alone.

The strategy the Americans employed appeared to be a good one. Like coaches before a game, the commanders looked at the opponent's weaknesses and planned accordingly to exploit those weaknesses with their own strengths.

The game plan was broken down as follows: Operation Pipestone Canyon would begin with two Marine battalions, BLT 1/26 and 3/5, attacking eastward into the operational area. This was designed as a feint, like a quarterback faking a handoff to the running back. These two battalions would then establish blocking positions on the railroad track that separated Da Nang from Go Noi Island.

After putting this zone defense in place, five American and South Vietnamese battalions would join forces and attack southward into Dodge City itself, then through to Go Noi Island. This phase was coordinated with two Korean Marine Corps battalions who joined the team. The Koreans were to hold positions on the southern edge of the area of operation. It was a good strategy on paper, but would it really hold up under the reality to come?

When the bombardment overhead ended, Danny eased himself off the ground. He turned to his men and said, "Alright, let's move out!"

Danny walked point on the left flank, away from the main column, with his Squad. They formed a long, single-file line as they slowly humped their way toward Dodge City — and the enemy. The darkness was everywhere. Danny thought again how much easier, and safer this would be during the day.

They had only walked a few hundred yards into the lowlands of the "Arizona" territory when a ground explosion rocked the night sky. "Corpsman!" screamed a Marine in the near distance. Danny instantly knew what had happened. That was the first of more than one hundred casualties the Marines had that night as a result of enemy booby traps and mines.

Danny slowly and cautiously inched his way forward, one step after another. His eyes scanned the ground for any sign of a booby trap. Can you imagine how hard it was to see a hidden booby trap in the pitch black? The fact was, you really couldn't see. Every step was like waiting to get your legs blown off.

Right behind Danny were his three Fire Teams. The Greek, Wells, and Combat led them. Danny silently prayed for daylight to come soon. As it finally came, Danny and his squad formed back up with the other Marines nearby, and the march continued toward Go Noi Island. On the march with the Marines were several M-48 tanks. Danny motioned with his left arm for his squad to follow him. He caught up to one of the tanks and climbed aboard the hull. His men did the same. The underbelly of a tank can withstand a booby-trapped explosion much better than the human body.

A few hours passed without incident; then they began to encounter heavy resistance from the tree line. The enemy had embedded itself and was firing at will on the Marines.

"Down! Get down!" yelled Danny. Danny and his squad dropped down into the moist ground and began firing back. Other squads did the same. After several intense firefights, the Marines finally quieted the resistance in the trees — but at a heavy cost. Several Marines lost their lives in those intense skirmishes.

Just like life, the march continued. Each step through the dense vegetation got them closer to their objective. As Danny's squad was nearing the tree line, there came the sound of gunfire, and the Greek suddenly went down.

"Hit the ground! Sniper!" yelled Danny. "Return fire! Return fire!"

As the squad opened up on the unseen enemy in the tree line, Danny low-crawled to his friend. Danny's heart clung to his throat as he saw that the Greek was motionless. "Corpsman up," yelled Danny. "I need a Corpsman over here!"

Danny rolled the Greek over on his back and began searching his body for bullet wounds, but he couldn't find any. Surprised by the intimate body search, the Greek quickly opened his eyes and said, "What the hell are you doing, Dan Bo?"

"Man, I thought you were dead. I was searching for bullet wounds."

"I'm ok," said the Greek. "But something hit me." He rolled up on his knees, took off his backpack and began examining it. He found a bullet hole through it. The sniper's bullet had luckily been stopped by the Greek's medal entrenching tool. "No. Man, they'd better not have . . ."

He quickly opened the pack and pulled out his stuffed koala bear. "Arggg! Look at it. They shot my koala bear!" He pulled the string, and the toy bear tried to speak, but its recording sounded more like a broken Alvin and the Chipmunk record. "Those commie ba***rds!"

The Corpsman finally reached their location. "Who's hit? Who's wounded?"

"No one, sir. We're good, but my bear got hit," said the Greek, holding up the bear.

The Corpsman shook his head and with a smirk replied, "I should have known it was you Greek," as he low-crawled back the other direction. They all laughed for a moment and then the seriousness of the mission took over again. Greek had survived a sniper's bullet and death again.

Finally, Danny and the Marines reached their destination at the railroad tracks. The Marines dug in and built very deep foxholes, with sandbags ringing the rims. They had prepared their blocking position. In a few short days, five allied battalions would attack the enemy from the north and push them southward into the hands of Danny and the Marines.

Danny and his squad had set up shop in an old graveyard on the right flank. Their job was to protect that side if the enemy broke through the lines. The graveyard was an eerie place to set up camp. Death hovered all around — not a comforting feeling for Marines who had already seen so much death.

Danny lined his foxhole with several of the headstones. He felt bad desecrating the graves in that way, but those stones would form an extra barrier between him and the enemy bullets. If those death markers could save a life, then he was willing to use them.

After a few days, intelligence reported that the operation was going exactly as planned. The Viet Cong and North Vietnamese Army were retreating directly towards the Americans' location. The Marines prepared themselves for the approaching storm.

On the evening of May 30, 1969, as dusk was nearing, Danny checked in with his Fire Teams and gave them some last-minute instructions for the night. A new member had recently joined his Squad. His name was Gordon Dean Perry. He was twenty years old, and also from Danny's home state of West Virginia. Gordon lived in Morgantown, which was only about four hours from Danny's home in Huntington.

Danny took a liking to him immediately. How could you go wrong with another West Virginia boy in your squad? Danny took him under his wing and protected him as much as possible. Danny remembered what being a boot was like. No one wanted to be near an untested boot, so Danny assigned Gordon to his own foxhole, along with the Greek and Chicago.

Danny dreaded the approach of midnight. Why? Because unbeknown to his squad, May 31, 1969, was the day Danny dreamed would be his last on earth. More times than he wanted to admit, he had seen himself lying in a casket — not a fantasy, but a nightmare. So, as you can imagine, Danny was nervous and anx-ious about what fate this night had in store for him. At the same time, he wanted to get it over with. No matter what, he wasn't going to take this lying down. If he were going to die, then he would die — but he would go down fighting.

Danny volunteered for first watch as the others rested to the side of the foxhole. He wasn't going to sleep this night. His senses are on high alert. He gazed into the dark night waiting, wonder-ing, and knowing the gooks are crawling all around them looking for an American to kill. He knew that you couldn't hear them or see them until they are on top of you. All Danny could do is use his sixth sense. He knew when his skin started to chill and goosebumps came up on the back of his neck, it was time to get it on.

Next to him, the Greek, Chicago, and Gordon lightly dozed. Danny cradled a St. Christopher medal, even though he wasn't Catholic. Actually, he was a Baptist. A dying Marine had given it to Danny for safe-keeping. As he watched the life drain from his comrade, Danny committed to wearing the medal in his honor. Danny kept that medal near his heart from that day on as a reminder, not only for this fallen soldier, but also for all fallen soldiers in this terrible conflict.

As he sat there in the darkness, cradling that medal, Danny began to pray silently. "God, I know I haven't been a perfect man, but You know I have always rested on You. Boy, do I need that rest now. God, I don't want to die." Danny paused. As he did, he squeezed his pocket Bible in his left hand. This small Bible and the St. Christopher medal had calmed his weary soul on many occasions. "If I am to die tonight, then help me to die as a fighter. Give me courage. Please give me strength. I pray for my friends in this foxhole, too. Please protect us and all the soldiers. In Jesus' Name, Amen."

Danny sat there in the silence. It was close to midnight now, or a little after. No one really knew the exact time. What was the use? But he felt better after he spoke to God. He felt the peace of God. In that moment of peace, suddenly the world exploded around him. The enemy launched NVA B-40 rockets at the Marines. Danny instinctively yelled, "Incoming!" Marines every-where jumped into foxholes and prepared for the inevitable. Danny activated the claymore mines in front of their position. The enemy then opened up with everything they had. Along with the rockets came an avalanche of small arms fire as they charged forward. Danny activated the claymore mines in front of their position, dropping many of the charging suicide sappers. The trip wires set off the Marine illumination flares. Silhouettes of enemy soldiers were charging their position. Danny thought, "This is it. This is the time for me to die."

But he wasn't done yet. Using his M-79 grenade launcher, he pumped shell after shell into the enemy. Alongside him, the Greek, Chicago, and Gordon emptied magazine after magazine as they sent their own avalanche of bullets toward the enemy. Viet Cong bodies fell, one after another. But they kept coming. Where were they all coming from? What was the size of their force? The bullet-ridden headstones in front of Danny splintered under the punishment.

Danny looked to his right and saw that Gordon had been hit. Gordon slumped over, limp. As Danny went to help him, an NVA B-40 enemy rocket screamed through the air right towards them. Danny dove towards the ground as the rocket landed inches from him. He felt the hot shrapnel as it ripped into his back, legs, and head. The blast propelled Danny forward and he hit the ground hard. "Well," he thought. "This is it. Just as I had dreamed." He lay there for what felt like an eternity, but, in reality, it was only a few seconds. He then pulled himself up on his knees in a crouching position. "I may be about to die," he thought, "but I am going to help Gordon first."

Danny crawled over to Gordon, ignoring his own pain. He got no response out of Gordon. He searched for a pulse, but found none. Danny hated this war. He hated the gooks. He knew he shouldn't call them that, but that was how he felt, and that was all that mattered at that moment.

All of a sudden, the fury jumped from Danny to Chicago. Chicago jumped up and, with a ferocious scream that Sasquatch would be envious of, he unleashed his enormous M-60 machine gun into the belly of the beast. The Greek threw some M-26 grenades out in front of their foxhole to clear the front of the kill zone.

As quickly as the battle began, it was over. Silence fell over the graveyard. A dense fog of smoke hovered six feet above the ground. The air smelled pungently of hot metal, sweat, and blood.

Danny and the Greek carried Gordon's lifeless body inside the perimeter to the Corpsman. The Corpsman took one look at Danny and the blood trickling down the back of his neck, head and legs. "You're hit too, Marine!"

"I know," said Danny. "Take care of this Marine." The Corpsman checked Gordon and knew instantly that he was gone. The moans of other wounded Marines enveloped the area. The Corpsman said to Danny, "Let me check your wounds."

Danny shrugged him off and said, "I am ok! Take care of those others first! They need you more than I do." Danny then sat down and checked himself closely. The wounds didn't seem to be life-threatening but they hurt just the same. Part of him was ecstatic; he had cheated death again. He had cheated the dream. He was alive! The other part of Danny felt tremendous sorrow for young Gordon and his family back home in West Virginia. He tried, but he couldn't protect Gordon. He tried with all he had, and Gordon died anyway. War is hell!

A medivac helicopter landed, and Gordon's body was placed on board. Then the other wounded Marines were also gently placed on board the aircraft. Gordon was the only Marine Killed in Action (KIA) that night. As a unit, they were lucky. But, for Gordon, his destiny ended here.

"Danny, you are wounded," said the Corpsman. "Get on that bird and get out of here. I wrote you up for a Purple Heart".

"No. I am staying," said Danny.

"Come on man! Go to Tokyo for a few weeks and heal up."

"No. I said I am staying," said Danny emphatically. "I am not leaving my squad. Besides, I have some payback for Charlie. You fix me up here."

The Corpsman just shook his head, knowing that he had run up against a brick wall. Danny's mind was set, and he wasn't moving. The Corpsman relented and began removing the shrapnel from Danny's head, back, and legs and stitched him up. Danny received his first Purple Heart for that night. That night he was supposed to die, but his heart, commitment, faith, and even a bit of luck had more to accomplish.

After the sun had risen, the Marines surveyed their surroundings. Numerous enemy bodies lay unmoving, mere feet from their foxholes. After examining them, Danny was sure he had found the one that killed Gordon. It was the one closest to their foxhole. Anger burned down deep in Danny's soul. He felt guilty — but all he could see was a monster in front of him. He wanted to kill him all over again. Danny closely examined the lifeless body of the dead enemy and searched for intelligence. He had been shot through the heart. His family would never see him again either.

The energy drained from Danny's legs, and he knelt beside the dead enemy. His heart opened to God's presence and he began to pray, "God, I don't know what I am feeling. I am confused why You allow so much senseless killing and death all around us. I am angry at You for allowing this awful war. I am also grateful that I didn't die tonight, but why Gordon? Did you send him as my Guardian Angel? He was only a kid like I was when I got here. Thank You, Lord for sparing me. I grieve for Gordon and his family. Please comfort them. In Jesus Christ's Name, Amen."

Danny rose to his feet and saw Marines a few yards away dragging dead VC to a freshly-dug shallow grave. Danny reached down and dragged the enemy soldier to his final resting place.

CHAPTER NINE

OPERATION PIPESTONE CANYON:
THE NOOSE TIGHTENS

DANNY LAY IN HIS HOSPITAL BED, GLANCING through the pictures, newspaper articles, and magazines that Chris had left for him, not fully comprehending that it had been 38 years since he was in Vietnam. He read story after story about himself: War Hero, Police Hero, Martial Arts Champion. He sat riveted by what he was reading and seeing — but with little recognition. It was as if the man he was reading about was a stranger.

He flipped to the next photograph in the stack. It was a picture of himself in full combat gear in Vietnam. Danny stared at the picture. It pained him to see it, but it was as if his eyes were drawn to it. He couldn't take his eyes off of it. Eventually, fatigue won out, and Danny slowly closed his eyes and drifted off to a deep sleep — and a dark place in the recesses of his mind.

The fire rained down from the nearby Vietnamese Village. Russian-made AK-47 rifles and rocket-propelled grenades obliterated the turf near Danny's feet. The Marines were sitting ducks for the enemy missiles coming toward them from the top of the mountain next to their compound.

Danny returned fire on the village with his M-60 machine gun. The enemy fired back, and Danny hunkered down in his bunker. He then popped up and fired again. In the exchange, the old lady went down — dead!

"Why! Why did she go out there and try to put the fire out in the middle of a firefight? Why! Oh, God, what have I done?"

"Mr. Lane! Mr. Lane! Are you ok?" a nurse said as she desperately attempted to shake Danny awake from the nightmare. With a jolt, Danny opened his eyes. He was bathed in sweat, and his heart was running the Kentucky Derby.

He struggled to look up at the nurse whose head was now just inches from his own. With a deep exhale, he said, "Yeah! Yeah!"

THE REST of the day and night of May 31st, 1969 was uneventful — which meant there were no NVA assaults. Danny had lived through his dream of dying, and could now focus totally on the tasks at hand: staying alive and leading his squad through the fire of Vietnam.

On the morning of June 1st, Danny rose a bit slowly, as could be expected. He was bandaged up and very sore and stiff from his wounds. He pulled himself up from his air mattress, which was placed strategically behind some tombstones. He and his squad went on patrol a short distance from the railroad berm. As they got closer to a bunker complex, enemy mortars and small arms fire rained down on them. They took cover and quickly asked for help from a couple of their accompanying M-48 Tanks. In a few short minutes, the skirmish was over. It didn't take long for the tanks' 90mm shells to do their job. When all was said and done, seven enemy soldiers lay dead, and the Marines captured an eighth wounded enemy combatant.

On June 5th, American airpower unleashed its fury on Go Noi Island and the enemy by dropping more than 750,000 pounds of explosives. The ground shook with the punishment and the enemy scattered in an attempt to survive the bombardment. As a result, the enemy broke into smaller groups in hopes of sneaking past the Marines and their blocking positions. For the next few nights, firefights were common occurrences for Danny and his squad.

On June 11th, things got even worse. They had already experienced several all-night assaults from the enemy. So far, the American lines stood strong. It was about midnight when the night went from a peaceful calm to a violent barrage of sound and action.

Danny's senses went on full alert as he heard a firefight to his right. It was 75 yards away, maybe 100 yards. The 3/26 Marine unit was taking on fire. The Third Battalion Twenty-Sixth Marines were brought in from the water to reinforce the Marine blocking positions on the railroad berm. These Marines had been stationed on a naval carrier in the South China Sea.

"Stay alert, boys," said Danny. "We may be next! We must hold this railroad berm."

A short time later, something strange happened. Danny and his squad began taking fire from their right; the same direction as the 3/26. That in and of itself wasn't too strange. What was out of balance was that Danny and his squad were taking fire from an American M-60 machine gun. The M-60 makes a distinct sound when it is fired — there was no mistaking this. It was an M-60. Why were they taking on friendly fire?

Danny and his squad took cover in their foxholes until they could figure it out. They didn't have to wait long, for they received word that the 3/26 had been overrun. "The 3/26 has been overrun," yelled Danny. "That may be our gun, but that sure ain't our guys shooting at us. Open fire on that position! Take out that gun!"

As soon as Chicago opened up with his M-60 on the position, Danny and his Marines began taking fire from NVA B-40 Rockets. Fortunately, they were off-target this time. Danny screamed, "Shut it down, Chicago. Don't let them key in on our position!"

It is always a military priority on both sides of the fight to take out the machine gun positions first, since these guns have a tremendous rate of fire. That is why a Marine machine gunner has the most dangerous job in the infantry.

At the same time all of this was going down, the enemy started charging Danny's lines. The Marines fought aggressively, and the enemy began to fall. Soon, all was quiet. The battle was over. They had held the railroad berm.

The 3/26 had many casualties, and the medivacs began to arrive on location. Slowly, the word came down on what had actually happened. It was reported that the 3/26's four-man Listening Post had been taken out. Evidently, the enemy was able to sneak up on them, and all four Americans' throats were slit. That is how the NVA had gotten hold of the American M-60 machine gun.

That was a night of horrors that put all the Marines on high alert and on high edge. Their nerves were stretched, but not severed. It was obvious now that the strategy had worked. The NVA and VC had nowhere to go but through Danny and the Marines. The NVA and VC were being pursued and pushed by the Korean Marines coming up on their six, leading the enemy right into the hands of Danny and the U.S. Marines. To Danny, however, it didn't feel like the enemy was handed to them on a silver platter. It felt more like they were the mice guarding the nest, while the NVA and VC were the hungry cat.

On June 12th, Danny and his squad were on high alert, sitting on pins and needles. It didn't help when a new, wet-behind-the-ears, First Lieutenant straight out of Quantico made a rash decision. The Lieutenant decided that Danny and his squad would go on an ambush mission that night in the same area that the 3/26 Marines had had their throats slit. The less-than-brilliant plan would send Danny's squad to the other side of the railroad berm right after dark. They were to sneak and slither their way out about two hundred yards and hide in the canopy until the enemy made a break toward the American lines. What this Lieutenant didn't understand, or was too green to care about, was that this trek would land them smack dab in the middle of a hornet's nest of embedded and trapped enemies. Talk about cornering a wounded animal!

Danny politely and firmly made his concerns known about this plan. The Lieutenant was having none of it; he was in charge and enforcing his authority. What he was really doing was committing Danny and his men to a suicide mission.

After the briefing, some of the members of Danny's squad made reference to "fragging" their new leader. Fragging was deliberately killing a fellow American soldier in cold blood. Unfortunately, this happened more times than you and I would like to think. Sometimes it was because of race, a disagreement, or what some might think of as survival of the fittest. Often the heat of battle was used as cover for such an attack. Who knows where an M-26 grenade might land as the battle rages?

Danny had several new Marines in his squad. He didn't know them very well yet, or their ability to act under fire. They were as green as this new CO. He did, however, have his veterans: the Greek, Combat, Wells, Chicago, and Rootie Poot.

One of the green Marines looked at Danny and said, "I ain't going out there, Corporal. That's suicide! That Lieutenant is full of sh**! He needs to take his own a** out there if he thinks that is such a genius plan. We should frag his a**! I'm not going out there! That's a death sentence!"

"That is alright," said Danny. "I will go in your place. This is my squad, and we will carry out the mission. We are Marines. We do as we are told. You know, you can be court-martialed for not following orders."

"I don't care. I am not going out there!"

"So you're refusing to fight? Is that what you are saying?" asked Danny bluntly.

"I'm not refusing to fight. I am just refusing to go out there tonight. Those gooks sliced those Marines' necks. I like my neck right where it is!"

"Ok, I'll have to brief the Lieutenant. It will be up to him on what happens to you now," said Danny.

"Do what ya gotta do, Corporal."

Danny went and briefed the Lieutenant on the situation with the new Marine. The new Marine was immediately put under military arrest and would be put on the next helicopter to the rear area, where he would face disgrace and a court-martial. There are some things worse than death — like cowardice.

Danny wasn't happy about the mission either. He didn't agree with it. He had also been in-country eight months, and only had five more months before he could go home. He didn't want to risk being killed by such a dumb plan. Not to mention his wounds, which got his attention every time he moved. But he was a Marine. He also was a leader now. He wasn't about to send his men into harm's way if he wasn't willing to go himself.

As dusk hung in the air, Danny and his squad very quietly moved towards their intended target. Rootie Poot was on point, Danny was behind him and the rest of the squad — minus one soon to be court-martialed new Marine — followed in his footsteps. The squad had more respect for Danny now than they had ever had before.

As the Marines neared their objective, a large explosion rocked the silence of the night. Then enemy AK-47 machine gun fire began raining down on them. All the Marines hit the ground and returned fire.

After a few intense minutes, the silence returned. The smell of gunpowder filled the night. The NVA had hit and then run. They had ambushed the Marines' ambush.

Danny yelled to his troops, "Headcount! Anybody hit?" They all knew what that meant. They began calling out, signifying their name and status — all of them except Rootie.

Danny looked deep into the smoke and darkness and saw the silhouette of Rootie a few yards from his location. "Rootie's down. I'm going to go get him. Stay put," called Danny.

Danny slithered his way like a snake across a damp lawn until he finally reached Rootie's lifeless body. There was no time to check for vitals. He quickly picked Rootie up, slung him over his shoulder, and started racing towards the perimeter. Bullets from the hidden enemy again filled the night sky as Danny's squad laid down cover fire.

Ever so close to the perimeter — but not close enough — Danny felt the hot lead of an enemy AK-47 bullet penetrate his right leg in mid-stride. He went down as the bullet burned through his insides. Danny urged his body back up like a boxer who had been knocked down. Out of pure determination and pigheadedness, he stood back up, got Rootie's body over his shoulder and ran toward the perimeter.

Once inside the perimeter, Danny locked eyes with the new Marine, who was in restraints. Danny didn't say a word; he didn't have to communicate more than the revulsion in his eyes towards that coward. Danny then looked into the face of the Lieutenant. The Lieutenant just stared at Danny with a locked jaw . . . silent.

Danny gently laid Rootie on the ground, and the Corpsman immediately came to his aid. The Corpsman took one look at the massive wounds on Rootie and knew it was already over. He looked up at Danny and slowly shook his head. "I am sorry, Corporal. He was dead as soon as the blast hit him."

"He saved our lives, particularly mine. I was right behind. Rootie took the brunt of the blast."

The Corpsman looked down and saw the blood running down Danny's leg. "Corporal, you're hit again. Let me take a look." Danny sat down as the Corpsman cut his pant leg up to examine the wound. "You're shot Corporal; I've got to get you out of here this time."

"Doc. I'll be ok. I can still walk as you see. Just shoot me up with some morphine and get that bullet out of me."

"Corporal, it's been less than two weeks since you got the other wounds. It's time for a vacation, you've earned it."

"You know the answer to that Doc. I ain't going anywhere unless I'm in a body bag."

The rest of the squad made it back inside the perimeter without incident. They were all saddened by the death of their comrade Rootie. They were also concerned, seeing the blood running down Danny's leg.

The corpsman took a closer look at the bullet wound on Danny's leg, cleaned it and gave Danny a feel-good shot of morphine. The Corpsman then went to work on Danny and removed the bullet. Fortunately, there was no damage to the bones or the major muscles.

"Here's your souvenir Corporal, courtesy of the NVA." The corpsman smiled.

As the medivac helicopter landed, the Corpsman said, "You sure you don't want to get on that bird and get out of here?"

"Doc, I don't want to get a taste of the good life and lose my edge. I'd rather stay in this hell until I can get out permanently. Besides, I have a squad to lead."

The Greek looked at Danny and said, "That is two Purple Hearts, Dan Bo. One more and you are out of here!"

"I know," said Danny. "I think I will pass on getting the third one. I'd rather not." A knowing smile creased the faces of these two close friends. The Greek knew exactly what Danny was saying, for he too had received two Purple Hearts.

Danny was awarded his second Purple Heart by the Corpsman for the wounds he received that night. The unfortunate thing is that the award would have been unnecessary, if not for a green Lieutenant who made an unwise decision. Rootie might be alive today if the Lieutenant had made a different decision.

The next day, June 13, Danny and his squad received new orders to protect a land-clearing company as the company leveled Go Noi Island. The idea was that if the island was a wasteland, then the VC and NVA would lose their safe haven and hiding place.

On the morning of the mission, the sun rose steadily in the Asian sky as Danny and his squad vigilantly looked on as the aerial bombardment began. It didn't take long for chaos to reign supreme. A deep, rumbling explosion rocked the peaceful beginning of the day. A second, third, and fourth explosion followed shortly thereafter. Enemy booby traps were the culprit again; Go Noi Island was infested with them. It was going to be a slow, dangerous, job to clear this island.

By late June, General Simpson had decided that America should have a permanent presence on the island. The plans were made to install two combat bases on the eastern side of the island. The western portion of the island would be taken care of by at least one Marine rifle company, who would secure it with continuous patrols.

After a few days of relative calm, intelligence reports indicated that the enemy had fled the area and sought refuge in the mountains and jungles of the Antenna Valley. Danny and his band of brothers were ordered to go after them. So much for the relative calm.

CHAPTER TEN

OPERATION DURHAM PEAK (ARIZONA TERRITORY & DODGE CITY ROUND #2)

DR. MCCOMAS STOOD AT THE END OF DANNY'S hospital bed, holding his medical chart. Several other doctors stood with him. Looking up from the records to the sleeping Danny, Dr. McComas said, "As you can see, Mr. Lane's condition is very complicated and quite perplexing. His brain has shut out reality, and appears to keep Mr. Lane in a loop of Vietnam in 1969. He is a war veteran, and appears to be suffering from Post-Traumatic Stress Disorder. His brain is swollen, and his spinal tap showed significant viral infection — although at this point it is unspecified. The nurse in charge last night heard him screaming, 'Fire for Effect.' She said he repeated it over and over, so she finally came in and woke him. She said he woke with a jolt and was very edgy and sweating profusely. I am concerned that his condition is getting worse and that our current regimen isn't working."

"If memory serves, 'Fire for Effect' is a military term for calling in artillery on the enemy position," said Dr. Garza. "He must have been experiencing a flashback last night. I suggest we continue pumping him with antibiotics to see if we can get that swelling down in his brain. If we can get on top of that, then we might just get him back to reality." The other doctors, including Dr. McComas, nodded in agreement.

Dr. McComas then walked to the side of the bed and gently touched Danny's leg in order to wake him. "Good morning, Mr. Lane. How are you feeling today?"

Danny fluttered his eyelids a couple of times, then said in a very dry, hoarse voice, "I'm okay."

"Very good, Mr. Lane. I am Dr. McComas. I am your doctor. I am here with some other doctors, discussing your situation. Do you know where you are?'

"Ahh, I don't know . . . No . . . I don't know . . . maybe Da Nang?"

ON JULY 20ᵀᴴ 1969, Danny and his squad were taken off Operation Pipestone Canyon and assigned to a new operation called Durham Peak. The goal of Durham Peak was to send Marines into the Antenna Valley, which was adjacent to the Que Son Mountains. This was about six miles south of their earlier position at An Hoa.

The terrain of this region could be quite daunting. The jagged peaks of the Que Son Mountains tower about 2,700 feet above the jungle canopy. The lowlands are carpeted with thick, densely-packed undergrowth, which is cut into an uncountable number of deep ravines — not a place you would want to go for a hike on a warm, sunny afternoon. But Marines go wherever they are sent.

Intelligence reports indicated that the enemy forces that fled the Americans at Go Noi Island and Dodge City had now embedded themselves in this treacherous region. It was time for Danny and the Marines to go and get them out.

As Danny and his team pushed southward into the mountain chain, they began to find evidence of the enemy. They discovered abandoned bunkers, hooches, supply caches, and even a few fresh graves. They were obviously on the right track. As they pushed further into the mountains, enemy resistance began to pop up. It was light initially, but then it began to intensify. The Marines were getting closer to the lions' den, and the lions weren't too pleased about it. As the hike continued, Danny felt as though he was having a little deja vu. The terrain looked very familiar, and for good reason: he had been there during Operation Taylor Common. The Vietnam War was a war of oddities — take this land, then give it back, then take it again.

On July 25, 1969, a platoon from Hotel Company took heavy sniper fire as they moved up a ridge finger leading to the peak of Hill 845. Enemy snipers on a rock ledge about one hundred meters above them plunked away at the Marines, dropping several with well-placed rounds. The platoon pulled back as an orbiting OV-10 Bronco loosed a barrage of rockets at the ledge. The snipers scattered.

The next day another platoon from Hotel Company returned to the area. An estimated company-sized unit of NVA ambushed them as they neared the battle site. The enemy was dug in along one side of the route. Because the dense foliage restricted visibility, the enemy aimed right along the ground, hitting the Marines in the lower legs. As the wounded Marines lay writhing on the jungle floor, an NVA sharpshooter shot them in the head or back. Six Marines were killed, and sixteen were wounded before the platoon could pull out of range.

In the confusion of the fight, the platoon's exact position could not be determined. Artillery was fired at the supposed enemy location but proved to be nearly a kilometer off. Rescue efforts faltered. While a medivac helicopter waited, it was shot down. A platoon of Marines had to be diverted from the original rescue attempt in order to secure the crash site. Finally, though, the lost platoon was located. The relieving force held off the enemy while the casualties were pulled to safety through the trees. Then the two platoons moved out to join the rest of the company near the summit of Hill 845.

There was so much unnecessary death and sacrifice for no logistical reasons. Taking a hill that they didn't need and then giving it back was the usual deadly military plan. It made no sense to the Marines in the bush. It was demoralizing to Danny and the foot soldiers, but they followed orders — sometimes deadly orders.

The mission continued for three long weeks. Every day was the same. It began to get monotonous — hike every day, search for the enemy, then dig in at night. It was like going to a mundane job, only to get up and do it all over again the next day. The only difference here was that people kept trying to kill him, and he never got a break.

In the jungles of Southeast Asia, the Marines never had the opportunity to go home at night and relax in front of the television set. Instead, they had "live theater" every night, where the actors were the Viet Cong and NVA, breathing down their necks. This particular theater did have a short run, though. The mission didn't go as planned. It was almost impossible to find the enemy in the dense jungle canopy. They were so well concealed and dug in that it was a suicide mission just trying to find them. Durham Peake was not being successful, and was called off on August 13th. Danny and his squad were then put back on Operation Pipestone Canyon to help the 7th Marines clear out the rest of the enemy near Da Nang.

In late August 1969, Danny and his squad were back in the Dodge City area of the Quang Nam Province. He was able to find a few quiet moments where he could gather his thoughts. He decided he would write a letter to his high school buddy, Darrell, to catch him up on what had been happening in his life. Danny pulled out a piece of paper and began to write. He had just enough time to write the letter and send it out on the helicopter that had dropped off their supplies.

Darrell,

Sorry I haven't written you since I have been over here. I am getting close to making it out of this hellhole at the end of the year. I am getting weary, tired, and weak. My mind is numb, and I really don't know what day or month it is most of the time. I would love to be there with you, shooting a game of pool, eating a baloney sandwich, and drinking a cold beer at Ms. Moon's Tavern.

Battling the VC and NVA is a cat-and-mouse game every day and night. It is discouraging, demoralizing, and exhausting. I have been here over ten months now, and have been in five major Military Operations! We kill thousands of them, and we lose hundreds of Marines on every mission. Everyone's life here is expendable. No one cares! You're just a number, and if you are killed, someone takes your place.

I have dodged bullets, rockets, mortars, booby traps, and even fought hand to hand. I am always wondering how many more times I have before I am one of the death statistics.

I have two Purple Hearts now. Just shrapnel from a rocket and a gunshot from an AK-47, not a big deal. I could have had a dozen if I had gotten written up for one every time I was injured during combat.

If I get another Purple Heart, I will be sent out-of-country. Marines go home after being wounded three times. Many times, though, that third Heart is deadly, so no one wants it! I don't!

The days seem like months, and months seem like years. I forget what a normal life is all about. I don't know what is going on in the world outside of this hellhole. I've walked by the same foxholes I dug months ago, during other engagements. People die here every day. I don't even know their names.

We aren't gaining ground. We aren't making progress. Some politicians are pulling our strings, and the commanders have to answer to them with a progress report. They have to report that we are winning the war and that we are motivated. What else are they going to say? I feel we are pawns being used for someone else's needs. The only reason we fight so hard is because that is the only way out. We fight for each other. Marines have a bond that is stronger than brothers. Makes you want to join the Marines, doesn't it?

It is hard to say that things here are routine, but war is that way. It's amazing that the human brain can finally accept the norm of any situation, just to survive.

I have lost contact with my previous life and who I was. I have lost contact with the real world and America. We have no television or news here, no paper, no phones, nothing. Just life in a hole in the ground every night, waiting for some guys named Charlie and wondering if that night is your last.

I feel like an old man in a young man's body. I have lost about 50 pounds, and I have migraine headaches every day. I have the stress of dying and the stress of trying to stay alive.

Please save this letter for me if I make it back, buddy. I should get out of here and arrive home by the end of the year. Tell the guys I said hello.

Your pal,
Danny

THE GREEK'S DESTINY WITH DEATH

September 8th, 1969, Danny and his squad were still in the Dodge City area on a sweep and destroy mission. They were providing security for the construction crews that were leveling the area for civilian habitation. Contact had been sporadic with Charlie as the area was almost leveled.

The Greek, Combat, and Wells would on occasion go out with some of the other rifle teams if needed. On this particular day, the Greek, Combat, and Wells volunteered to go with Kilo Company on a search and destroy patrol. For some unknown reason, Danny tried to talk them out of it. He felt uneasy about it.

"Greek, why risk getting yourself killed now, we are almost out of here. We've only got three months left." Danny pleaded.

"Ah, Dan Bo, I am bored man, those commie bas***** can't kill me, you know that." the Greek replies.

"Yeah, you have said that a thousand times and all it takes is that one bullet with your name on it to wipe your ass out." Danny preached.

"Ah, those gooks can't spell my name, Dan Bo. I'll be alright."

Danny, seeing he wasn't getting anywhere, wished him, Combat, and Wells a safe mission.

Kilo Company patrolled that day without incident and finally settled in about a half click (.3 tenths of a mile) away from Danny's position. As the dark of night hastened its entrance, Danny heard small arms fire a short distance away and knew it was coming from the direction of Kilo Company.

The Americans returned fire, and the night sky lit up with tracer bullets and explosions. Danny felt helpless from his position. All he could do was watch. Danny squinted and peered into the dark. His gut told him his eyes were telling the truth; Kilo Company was getting hit and hard. NVA B-40 rockets were heard penetrating the Kilo compound. After a few minutes, it was over as fast as it all began. The VC and NVA were notorious for their hit and run tactics.

The short-lived battle was over, at least for now. Danny looked deep into the distance, but all he could see was smoke and haze coming from the direction of Kilo Company. About twenty minutes later, he glanced up as he heard the roar of a helicopter soar overhead. That could only mean one thing. Wounded — or dead. Was the Greek among them? Danny hoped not.

Waiting was never Danny's strong suit; he was a man of action. But action couldn't give him the information he sought. The only way to discover the whereabouts and health of the Greek was to wait until he could return to the rear area and look at the MIA (Missing in Action) and KIA (Killed in Action) lists — or, by luck or happenstance, run across Kilo Company and ask them.

The next day, Danny and his squad of Marines were traversing the rice paddies when they came across another Marine unit. You can imagine Danny's relief and trepidation when he discovered it was Kilo Company. As Danny and his unit passed, he looked into the faces of the Kilo Marines, searching for his friend. Not just a friend, but a brother. The Greek and Dan Bo had been together since boot camp. They were family.

His instincts told him something was terribly wrong. The Greek was nowhere to be found. Danny yelled to some nearby Marines resting beside a dike, "Hey! Anyone know where the Greek is?"

"Yeah. Sorry, man. He's KIA. He got shot in the back last night during the firefight, then an RPG (rocket propelled grenade) landed in their hole."

"Oh my God!" Danny screamed.

"Killed him and f***ed the other two dudes up! The LZ was hot and his body dropped off the medivac and hit the ground as it took off. They had to come back down to get him."

The news hit Danny harder than anything else in his life. Harder than his mother's abandonment. Harder than watching his stepdad die in his arms. Harder than... anything.

"Are you sure he was KIA?" Danny asks.

"Yeah man, no way he could have survived all that." The Marine answers.

"What about my other men, Combat and Wells?" Danny asks.

"They got on the medivac too, not sure their condition. Didn't look good though"

"Thanks man." Danny states as the men in Kilo Company moves on.

Danny was numb and somewhat in disbelief, but helpless to do anything about it. He sat down, closed his eyes, and in deep thought prayed to God for strength and understanding.

"Why God!? Why the Greek! Why not me? Is there no limit to pain and suffering we have to go through? I need the strength to carry on Lord. I am about to my end. Show me, Lord, what I have to live for. I need some answers. In Jesus name, Amen."

Finally, God spoke to Danny. "Your job is not complete, and your purpose in life is not fulfilled yet. Finish your mission and carry on, Marine."

Danny made a decision at that very moment. After the war — that is, if he made it home alive — he was going to go to Cleveland and pay his respects to Sophia and the Greek's family. He would take the Greek's personal belongings and the Greek flag to his family. That was the least he could do for his best friend. He had God's instruction to carry on and finish his mission.

Danny would re-focus and stay sharp and diligent. With the grace of God, he would carry on — not alone, but being a leader of other young Marines until his journey ended.

Danny was a short timer now, and so many soldiers died when their time in-country was short. Many times, short timers made mistakes because they hesitated during battle and didn't take the risks they took when first in-country. Danny resolved not to let that happen to him.

The next two months went by at a snail's pace. Danny had to lead his squad into combat without his brothers, the Greek, Combat, and Wells. He didn't know if Combat and Wells were dead. To come this far and share life and death with these Marines was crushing to Danny's mindset, but Marines are taught not to grieve or let emotions take them over. Danny had new Marines to train and to try and keep alive.

There were many more combat engagements with Charlie in the Dodge City area the next two months. Searching and destroying the enemy was routine now. Every day was a game of life or death for someone on either side. The days seemed like months and the months like years to Danny, but he finally got the call to come back to An Hoa. Operation Pipestone Canyon was terminated on November 7, 1969.

The Marines had driven the enemy out of Dodge City and Go Noi Island. In all 852 enemies were confirmed killed, 58 captured plus 410 weapons and some impressive food caches. USMC losses were 71 KIA and 498 WIA. Now it was getting close to time for this Marine to go home.

CHAPTER ELEVEN

TIME TO GO HOME

"INCOMING! INCOMING!" DANNY SCREAMED as massive amounts of debris sprayed into the air. Danny lay flat on his belly and put his hands palm-down on top of his helmet to hold it in place. The high-pitched whine of more inbound 140mm rockets could be heard approaching the Marine compound. Danny and other Marines scrambled for the nearest fortified bunker.

The Russian made rockets were walking through the compound destroying everything and everyone in sight. The huge ammo dump exploded sky high as giant shards of metal flew through-out the compound.

"Mr. Lane! Mr. Lane! Wake up!" said a concerned nurse as she fervently shook Danny awake. Those screams in the night were becoming a frequent occurrence from Danny's hospital room — but their regularity made them no less disconcerting, at least to the nursing staff.

Danny jerked straight up in bed in a cold sweat. The nurse gently laid her hands on each of his shoulders. "It is okay, Mr. Lane. You are here in the hospital. It is time to take your medicine." Danny quickly scanned the room for danger and then locked eyes with the nurse, whose head was mere inches from his own. The tension and stress seemed to ooze out of his body as he came to some recollection of his surroundings.

DANNY WAS IN the bush on a sweep and destroy mission near An Hoa with Mike Company 3/5 when word came from the Commanding Officer that Danny was going home. It was mid-November, 1969 and Danny had been in-country for twelve months and, in a matter of days, he would be back stateside. Danny could hardly believe it. It seemed like an eternity since he had been home in West Virginia.

Later that same day, Danny climbed aboard a helicopter which took him back to An Hoa, so that he could prepare to go home. Back at An Hoa, Danny was told that he had to wait two days before being sent to Da Nang. From Da Nang, he would be transferred home.

Anxiety, like he had never experienced before, began to well up inside of him. He had made it this far, and didn't want to get struck out in the bottom of the ninth inning. He had heard of so many guys who were about to go home, but got taken out by a freak rocket or random attack. He wasn't going to let that happen to him if he could help it. And it could happen; An Hoa was still under constant attack.

That night, Danny found the largest, deepest, and most heavily-fortified bunker and decided to make it his home for the night. It was the Taj Mahal of all bunkers. It was huge and fortified like Fort Knox. Danny thought to himself, "It is perfect!" That is, as long as he didn't get found out. It must have been the bunker for the commanding officers, but Danny snuck in and made himself at home. I can't say it was a restful night for Danny, but at least it was a safe night. Until this writing, no one ever discovered that Danny had been in that bunker. For, you see, he was the only one in that bunker that night — and that was fine with Danny.

Danny sighed with relief when the sun poked itself through the openings in the bunker. He got up and began preparing his gear and personal belongings. One more day, and he was out of there. You can imagine Danny's shock when the Commanding

Officer assigned him to bunker watch that night. Bunker watch at An Hoa took place right on the front lines, which were no picnic. The enemy constantly harassed the American lines in an attempt to break through.

Danny protested to the CO, "Sir, this is my last day here. I am going home tomorrow."

The CO looked at Danny with disgust and said, "Marine, I don't give a crap. You are still here. You are a Marine until you are discharged. You will do bunker watch duty tonight. Report at 1900. Is that clear?"

"Yes, sir."

At 1900, Danny reported as ordered. He was assigned to what the Marines called the mini-fortress. The mini-fortress was the front line of defense for the main compound. The Marines had positioned barbed wire in front of the bunker to slow down any frontal attack from the enemy, as well as trip flares and claymore mines around their position. The bunker was also heavily sandbagged, but Danny would have preferred his Taj Mahal from the night before.

Danny didn't want to deal with this crap tonight. He had one stinking night left. One night! Why would the CO do this to him? Two of the three other Marines with Danny that night felt the exact same way, for they, too, were short timers. So, here they were: three short timers and one other Marine. Who was this other Marine? Only a fresh behind the ears, barely out of puberty, just arrived in-country "boot."

The four Marines settled in for the night. Danny discovered that the "boot" was from his home state of West Virginia. They chatted for a few minutes about home, then readied themselves for what was to come. Danny really wanted a quiet night. He prayed for it. But no matter what was to come, Danny knew that God was with him and everything would be okay, no matter the result.

Danny told the other Marines to try to get some sleep. He would take watch. He wasn't about to shut his eyes that night; he was going to stay awake and alert. They had a huge M-60 machine gun mounted on the front of the bunker. Danny checked it to make sure it was good to go in case he needed it. They also had a Star Light scope, which was a crude form of night vision specs — but it was state-of-the-art in 1969. Danny kept his eyes peeled with the Star Light, scanning the entire countryside in front of their position.

Danny sat there in the dark and pondered all that he had been through in the last year. How he had survived, he would never know. Except for the grace of God, he would be dead like the Greek. Danny's reflections and the quietness of the night were abruptly shattered. About a click away, the night sky lit up like Independence Day with an all-out assault by the NVA and the VC. Again, it was Kilo Company that was taking the brunt — for the moment. After about five minutes, silence again ruled the night. An eerie silence, like the stillness of the trees before a tornado rages.

Danny looked intently through the scope. He saw something, but it might be nothing. Quite often, you would get a false reading from the scope. It would sometimes pick up light reflection from the moon or other low light sources. Squinting even more intently, Danny scanned their position again. There it was again; something was out there, about 100 feet away. It might be the enemy, or it might be a rock ape. Either way, the pit in the bottom of his stomach began to grow. There — he saw it again. Multiple bogeys. It had to be men. The motions were too fluid for a rock ape. Yes! He was sure of it. The attack was headed their way.

Danny woke up the other Marines in his foxhole. He then picked up the radio and said, as quietly as he could, "Command, we have movement in front of our position. Multiple bogeys. Ten, maybe fifteen."

"Roger," said Command. "Hold your fire until they all get in the barbed wire in front of your position."

"Roger," Danny replied. He then set the radio down and said to the other Marines. "I am not too comfortable waiting that long. The sappers are often wired with explosives. I am not about to get blown up on my last night. If I am going to go, then I am going on my own terms."

Danny peered out again into the hazy night. He thought to himself, "If there are that many in front of our bunker, then how many are out there altogether?" He then looked at his fellow Marines who were sitting stiffly beside him. All of their senses were on high alert. Danny locked eyes with the boot, and saw terror in his eyes. Danny remembered that look — and that feeling. He gave the boot a quick nod of the head and said, "Alright. I am not waiting any longer. Let's light them up!" Danny picked up the radio again and said into the handset, "Command, I am going to commence firing!"

"Roger," said Command. "Let me coordinate with other positions. Wait for countdown."

A few seconds passed, then command came back over the radio, "Commence firing in 3, 2, 1. . . FIRE!!!" All of a sudden, the Marines let loose from all locations. Danny was on the M-60, giving the enemy everything he had. The bullets were flying so fast out of the barrel that it became too hot from the friction and Danny had to replace it.

The enemy unloaded on Danny's bunker with their own fury of AK-47 bullets. The boot screamed and went down. Danny could tell instantly that he was gone, dead in his first firefight. No time to grieve now. Danny continued firing with the M-60, and the other short timers continued to fire with their M-16s. Danny then held up his hand, signaling for them to stop firing. All was quiet. Where was the enemy? Did they get them all, or were they playing opossum? Danny picked up the scope and looked intently around their position. He couldn't see anything. The air was filled with the smell of gunpowder and the smoke of Hades. The three Marines sat perfectly still for what seemed like an eternity. What should be their next move? Danny knew they needed to get the dead Marine to the Medivac. He also didn't want to move too much in case the enemy was still out there, lurking in the darkness.

They laid low inside the bunker and waited it out. Daylight couldn't come soon enough — and for Danny, it didn't. Minutes passed like hours.

When daylight finally arrived, Danny climbed out of the bunker and saw many dead VC and NVA sprawled out in the barbed wire mere yards from the entrance to the bunker. He thought to himself, "I made it! I am actually going to get out of here on a seat and not in a body bag."

Other Marines got the dead Marine from West Virginia to the compound for processing and transportation back to the world. He was a boot, new, and as green as Danny had been a year earlier.

A search of the dead enemy bodies revealed explosives, weapons and packages of opium and heroin on each soldier. It was normal and well known that the enemy was always charged up on something besides their communist cause. The drugs gave them the courage and the deranged mindset to go on these suicide missions. In all, there were sixteen bodies scattered throughout the barbed wire. Danny left the cleanup of carnage to other Marines as he had a ticket out of there.

A few hours passed, and Danny was all packed up and ready to go. He originally planned to be airlifted by helicopter to Da Nang but, again, things changed. His hopes of getting out of Vietnam alive hit a snag when he was told that, instead of the 'copter, he would be transported to Da Nang by a truck in a convoy. Not good news. Traveling by truck took an hour and a half through enemy territory, Dodge City, and the Arizona Territory. The only road was a constantly booby-trapped patch of dirt that had more bumps than a kid with the chicken pox. The Marines swept this road daily for mines, and Danny hoped they had been extra vigilant in the last twenty-four hours.

Danny spoke very little during that bumpy truck ride. In fact, he sat as low as he could in the back of that truck. The last thing he wanted was to make it through the last thirteen months, only to be taken out by an enemy sniper on his way to the airport in Da Nang. Since he had turned in his rifle before boarding the truck, he also felt very naked and vulnerable. Now he had to rely solely on the protection of the drivers in the front of the truck, for they were the only ones who were armed.

Well, I can't say it was an enjoyable ride through the countryside, but Danny made it to Da Nang safe and sound. Now all that was left was to board that plane and fly back to the rest of the world — to Camp Pendleton in sunny California.

CHAPTER TWELVE

ANOTHER SURPRISE BEFORE
LEAVING VIETNAM: THE USS IWO JIMA

DR. MCCOMAS AND SEVERAL OTHER DOCTORS stood around Danny's bedside. There was a hovering gloom in the room of St. Mary's hospital. Danny's son, Chris, and two of Danny's friends, Tim Koontz and Mark Underwood, also stood nearby. Both Tim and Mark were lawyers who were asked to help organize much of the legal paperwork involved in Danny's medical crisis.

"Gentlemen," started Dr. McComas. "I appreciate you coming on such short notice. We have a challenge here. Unfortunately, I have to inform you that we are planning to discharge Mr. Lane. There is nothing more we can do for him. As you know, he has tried to escape several times as of late. The other night, the police apprehended him for going down Third Avenue in his wheelchair. Just last night, he believed that he saw bad guys crawling up the side of the hospital, so he took it upon himself to call the SWAT team. That is five times this week alone that he has called 911!"

"But, Doctor, doesn't that show progress with his memory?" asked Tim, like he was cross-examining a witness. "At least he has stopped calling in artillery. Now, he is reliving his days as a cop. That is a move in the right direction from a time perspective."

Dr. McComas looked down at Danny and exhaled before his spoke. "I know you all care for Danny very much. I do too, but my hands are tied. I have to discharge him to make room for other patients. He has no insurance except for the Veterans Health Administration, and so far, they have not agreed to pay for the cost of his care or approve a transfer to their facility."

"So we are really talking about money, aren't we?" asked Mark.

"Look, I'm sorry. We aren't equipped to help him here anymore. We don't know what the real problem is. He needs a neurological expert, someone who specializes in memory loss, brain infections, and this kind of trauma. I recommend you take him to the Mayo Clinic in Minnesota. I can send all his records there for you. At this time, Danny needs around-the-clock care and a surrogate to work on his behalf. He can't even walk on his own yet. And, quite frankly, he can be dangerous. The man is a highly trained Marine and martial artist. Combine that with his brain infection, and you have a disaster waiting to happen. We are fortunate he hasn't hurt anyone… yet. Let me be blunt; we don't know if he will recover from this ailment. In fact, it could kill him. I see that he has only two options besides the Mayo Clinic."

"What are those options, doctor?" asked Chris.

"Well, either send him to live at a nursing home or take him home."

"A nursing home? That is awful! Look, I can't be with him twenty-four hours a day. I am in college, I have a job, and a new baby. There are no other family members that can be with him all day. But a nursing home is unacceptable. You can't do this!"

Dr. McComas was grieved at this discussion. He hated this part of his job. He went to medical school to be a healer, but he knew that not every patient could be healed . . . at least, not by human hands.

"I will draft the Surrogate and Power of Attorney documents for Chris," said Mark. "I will send a notice to the VA letting them know that I represent Danny. His condition is obviously a result of his military service, and they need to provide compensation for these bills. They also need to provide him further medical attention. I will fight the VA until I get some reasonable results."

"Ok," said Dr. McComas. "I agree. That sounds reasonable. I am sorry that it has come to this and that I couldn't be of more help to him. I will sign the release papers, and you men can sign him out. I do wish him the best."

AFTER ARRIVING at the 1st Marine Division at Da Nang, November 21st, Danny waited in line to turn in his paperwork. He could hardly believe it. He had made it alive — he was going home! He would be home within two days. When he got to the front of the line, he handed his paperwork to the clerk. After a few moments, they handed Danny his processed papers for the trip home.

Danny glanced at them, and immediately the muscles in his jaw relaxed as his mouth fell open in shock. He looked at the clerk and said, "I am supposed to fly home."

"That is not what it says, Corporal. You will be traveling home on the USS Iwo Jima." The clerk then motioned for the next soldier to bring his paperwork forward. Danny stepped out of line with a wave of emotions running through his entire body. The Marines had flown him over to Vietnam in a day, and now, *now* it was going to take him a month to get home. Unbelievable! Thanks for serving your country.

Danny was part of a large troop withdrawal ordered by President Nixon. After waiting around another twenty-four hours, Danny and the other Marines were transported to the South China Sea, where the impressive aircraft carrier and troop transport the USS Iowa Jima sat docked. Danny had to admit; the ship looked almost majestic as it sat there in the sunlight. Pride welled up in him as he thought of the name of the ship — Iwo

Jima. That great, powerful ship was a monument to the men who lived and died on that hallowed ground some twenty-five years earlier.

Danny's enthusiasm took another turn for the worse when he learned the plan for embarking the ship. The press was going to be present, and, in order to make the event look good for the President, the troops were going to board the ship by climbing up the ropes slung over the side of the enormous vessel.

Danny almost didn't make it up that braided rope. He had lost a tremendous amount of weight in the last year, and he was weak and exhausted even before the climb. He pulled himself up over the rim of the ship and could barely stand. He was covered with sweat from the top of his head down to the hairs on his toes. The troops were then ordered to stand at attention in rows on the carrier deck. All this pomp and circumstance was for the birds; welcome to the world of politics.

As Danny stood there looking at the horizon, his eyes gazed upon the land that had been his home for the last twelve months. He hated that place. His jaw tightened as his memory raced through the past 365 days. He thought of the many battles, his two Purple Hearts, the gruesomeness of the war, the men who died, and particularly the loss of his best friend, Sotere.

"Why, God, why?" thought Danny. "Why did I live and Sotere died? What did we accomplish for all this? We took ground, and we gave it back. We then took it again — at a cost. Why? Oh God, why?" As he ended his prayer, this tough war veteran flicked a tear from his right cheek. For twelve months, Danny had held his emotions in check; for the most part, he chose not to feel. Now, he was beginning to feel human again.

As the coastline of Vietnam got smaller and smaller in the distance, Danny made a decision. He wasn't going to waste this opportunity. He was alive! He knew that God must have plans for him, and he was ready to pursue the next journey in his life, whatever that would be.

After all the pomp and circumstance had ended and Vietnam was just a speck on the horizon, Danny and the Marines started to file off the hangar deck and through the hatch that led to the interior of the massive ship. As Danny waited in the long line, another thought dawned on him: "What is there to do on an aircraft carrier for the next thirty days?" Well, Danny soon found out the answer to that question: not much. It also wasn't the brightest idea to coop up five hundred grizzled Marine combat veterans with thousands of sailors.

Danny discovered there were a few activities that you could do on an aircraft carrier. When planes weren't being launched from it, the Marines did jumping jacks on the deck. Soaking in the warm sunshine and not having to worry about being shot at was a nice change for the Marines.

Danny also joined some pickup basketball games played in the hull of the ship. It was humorous to see the Marines attempt to play ball as the massive ship swayed back and forth with the waves. It was as if they had each drunk a six-pack of beers before heading out onto the court. It was fun, even though it wouldn't have passed Coach John Wooden's approval for disciplined basketball.

Danny also got reacquainted with the television set. They had a closed-circuit TV on board, but they only had a few options to watch. They had one college football game, which they showed every day. After a while, the plays ran through his mind as he slept like sheep jumping over a fence. They also had several reruns of the popular program *Bonanza*. By the time they reached San Diego, Danny could quote "Little Joe" word for word. The one show that went over like a 102-degree fever on a four-year-old was the John Wayne Vietnam movie, *The Green Berets*. After living the real deal, the Marines couldn't stomach the glossed-over Hollywood version.

But the one thing that the Marines and Sailors alike will never forget about that journey was the mysterious rash. It showed up after about a week out at sea. Before picking up the Marines in Southeast Asia, the ship had been docked at Hong Kong. Evidently, the ship had taken on some little stowaways; tiny crabs had boarded the cruise and were having the time of their lives. The ship was infested with the little parasites. They chewed incessantly on the Marines and the Sailors alike. They weren't picky. Danny itched all over, then the redness began to burn. His skin felt and looked like an over-ripened raisin on a sunny day. Thank you, US Navy, for your hospitality.

AFTER TWENTY-THREE long days in St. Mary's hospital, the doctors discharged Danny to his son Chris. They had decided that his case was too complicated for their staff, and couldn't help him any more than they had.

Chris was legally named his surrogate and given power of attorney over all of his affairs. The VA still wouldn't take responsibility for Danny. Chris didn't want him put in a nursing home, so taking him home was his only option. The hospital did get Danny an appointment at the Mayo Clinic in Minnesota in January 2007 for more advanced neurological tests.

The problem was, Chris would have to pay to fly his dad there, get a hotel and stay with him for a week of tests. The Mayo Clinic had also demanded a $5000 deposit just to confirm the appointment, and Danny would be liable for all tests and doctor fees. The estimated cost of travel, hotel, and medical tests totaled more than $25,000.

That was an impossible option, as Danny simply didn't have that kind of money at that time. It was tragic what was happening to this warrior. There was little hope for his recovery and not enough money to get advanced medical help.

Chris would now have the weight of the world on his shoulders, going to college, working a part-time job, taking care of his father, and being a new dad. Chris' new son Eli had just arrived into the world a few days previously.

A shell-shocked Chris finally left the hospital with his dad, a big bag of prescriptions pills, and a walker. Chris got his dad in the car and drove towards home. Danny glared out the window puzzlingly, trying to piece together what was happening to him.

Danny's home at that time was a huge two-story with four bedrooms, three baths and a nice swimming pool in the rear. Danny was living there protecting the home for a former client he represented in a private eye case. The home had been taken over by Detroit drug dealers, and his client had been kidnapped and was being held hostage. When the drug dealers demanded ten thousand dollars or the client would be killed, Danny was called in by the family to help rescue their son. Danny dropped off the ransom money, called in SWAT, and got their son back. The client was currently out of state in protective custody awaiting the trial of his kidnappers.

Chris had many concerns. What was going to happen when he was at college, work or seeing his new son? Should he hide his dad's guns? Should he hide the car keys? How was he going to keep his dad retained from leaving again?

As darkness approached on this first day home, Danny became more and more anxious. His breathing became labored, and he got edgy. He got up and used the walker to go look outside. It was pitch dark except the dim light from the street lights. Flashes of silhouettes ran through Danny's mind. Danny closed all the blinds on the windows. In a panic, he went searching for his guns, but he couldn't find them. He believed there were people after him that wanted him dead. He grabbed a butcher knife off of the kitchen counter. Chris had left him his cell phone with his number on speed dial. Delirious, he called Chris.

"Yeah Dad, you ok?" Chris answered.

"Where are you?" Danny asked in a panic.

"I told you Dad; I was coming to see my son, Eli, your grandson."

"Where are my guns?"

"I can't let you have your guns Dad; you know that. Are you ok? You are breathing heavy and seem to be in a panic."

"I need my guns! There are people out there that want to kill me! It's dark, and bad things happen in the dark."

"The war has been over for forty years, Dad."

"It's never over, son!"

"You are not in Nam or a cop anymore, Dad! No one wants to kill you! I will be home in a while, try to relax."

"Where's my car keys?"

"You can't drive Dad! You know that! Calm down. I'll be home in a few minutes."

Chris hangs up the phone as Danny lies down on the couch and tries to slow down his breathing. He has a death grip on the butcher knife in his right hand.

ON DECEMBER 21ST, 1969, after thirty long days at sea, the massive vessel drifted slowly into the San Diego Naval Yard. Over five hundred Marines stood on the upper deck, anxiously anticipating the glory and honor of stepping back on American soil.

As Danny and the other Marines disembarked on that warm, sunny California day, they thought there would be some sort of a reception parade, lots of cameras, and a big hoopla. After all, they were American heroes, were they not? They had fought the good fight for God and their country. They had heard the call to duty, and they had answered that call.

But . . . there was nothing. No parade. No news cameras. No people cheering and welcoming them home. There was simply . . . nothing.

The Marines were herded into the back of cattle cars repurposed for troop transport and hauled off to Camp Pendleton for combat debriefing and orientation back into civilian life or, in some cases, their next military assignment.

Danny and his fellow Marines went through a battery of tests to determine if they were ready to transition back into society. From a physical standpoint, Danny weighed in at a whopping 130 pounds. When he joined the Marine Corp, he had weighed 180 pounds. However, the Vietnam heat, malaria, and lack of proper nutrition on the battlefield had sucked those fifty pounds right off his body.

From a psychological standpoint, the Marine Corp wanted to make sure that they weren't unleashing homicidal maniacs back into an unsuspecting society. As you can tell, there wasn't much known about Post-Traumatic Stress Disorder back in those days. And there wasn't much compassion for the war veteran who had escaped the gates of Hades. Escaped? Yes. But not unscarred.

Danny soon learned that you answered "yes" to all the head doctor's questions — that is, if you wanted to be seen as normal and ready for society. In reality, he wasn't ready to acclimate back into society. And who would be? Danny had been in combat more than 300 days during his tour. In comparison, the average soldier in World War II saw around 40 days of combat.

Danny had seen hundreds of soldiers shot dead or blown apart right beside him. Some of them were men he knew and cared for. He had carried their lifeless forms back to safety. Danny had killed the enemy, sometimes from afar and sometimes up so close that he could smell their breath. Was he ready for society? No. And, again, who would be?

Danny finally got some leave from the base after he was deemed fit to be in society. He went with a few Marines to a local club to listen to some much-missed music. He also craved a good, cold beer. The doorman asked for an ID and Danny showed him his Marine dog tag.

"Listen, kid," said the burly bouncer. "I need an ID with your age on it."

Danny handed the bouncer his ID, and the man threw it back at him. "You're not old enough to get in here, kid. So beat it!"

"Man, I just got back from Vietnam. I have been over there for two years."

"Kid, that doesn't mean anything! If you aren't twenty-one years old, then you aren't getting in here. I said, beat it!"

Danny was old enough to fight for his country and kill people in war, but not old enough to drink a beer in the state of California. Something just didn't seem right about that.

Danny had brought back two AK-47 machine guns as souvenirs. He had picked them up from dead NVA whom he had killed. Marines were allowed to bring two enemy weapons home that they had confiscated during battle. He sold both guns for a total of $650 to other stateside Marines. He then took the money and bought a black market Marine ID. Danny Lane was now William Hellbig, a twenty-one year old who was allowed to drink beer in the United States of America.

For the next few nights, Danny put that fake ID to good use. He got to know the night life of Oceanside, California quite well. It felt good to listen to music, drink some beer, and relax after surviving the war.

Something that did plague his mind during these days was what would he do after he got home to West Virginia. What did he want to do with the rest of his life?

After passing all the post-war medical tests, Danny was given two options for his future. One, he could stay in the Marine Corp and be promoted to Sergeant and be stationed in Spain. Or two, he could have an early release from active duty because he had seen combat and had received two Purple Hearts. Danny chose option two and made plans to go home to Huntington, West Virginia to finish his stint in the Marine Corps Reserves.

Finally, the day arrived when Danny would fly home. He woke up extra early with anticipation on that December day. As he showered, shaved, and put on his green winter dress uniform, his thoughts turned melancholy. Nobody even knew he was coming home to West Virginia — or probably cared. As he looked at himself in the mirror, he shook his head to rattle the gloom out of his attitude. Nothing was going to ruin this day for him. He was going home... HOME!

As the taxi cab rounded the bend, entering the San Diego airport, the motion caused the medals on Danny's uniform to clink together. He glanced down at the left side of his chest at all the medals and ribbons he had received for heroism. He was proud of his accomplishments and how he overcame adversity during the direst of circumstances. He knew he was ready for whatever the future had in store. He could conquer anything.

Danny stepped out of the cab and handed the driver some cash. "Thanks," said Danny. The cab driver just glared at him and said nothing. Danny thought this odd, but decided the guy must just be in a bad mood. In his mind's eye, Danny envisioned fellow passengers and the flight crew cheering him on and thanking him for his service.

As Danny made his way to the front of the line for check in and handed her his papers. The airline clerk said, "Military discount ticket huh? Well, soldier you have to wait until all the paying customers are on board. If there is an empty seat, you can fly with us."

"I just got home from the war ma'am. I really need to get on that plane." Danny responded.

"Like I said, soldier, you don't have any special treatment from us, so go over there and wait like I told you."

Where was the respect and honor that soldiers get when they come home from war? Danny wondered.

As Danny was waiting for the clerk to assign him a seat, a mother with her young son walked by. The kid was about Danny's age when he started paying with his little green army men. "Look, momma, a soldier! I want to be a soldier when I grow up momma."

"You don't want to be one of them son; they kill innocent people — and even kids." The mother quickly jerked her child by the hand and walked away quickly.

"There is definitely something going on," thought Danny. "Could it be that America isn't proud of their sons of war?" After all, he had received very little news from the world in over a year.

Danny boarded the plane without further incident. He found his seat and sat down. He nodded to the businessman who was seated right next to him. After a couple of minutes, the gentleman got up and headed toward the back of the plane. Danny thought the man had gone to the restroom before the plane took off, but the man never came back. Maybe he was sick. Danny only realized what had happened to the gentleman as he was lifting his duffle out of the overhead compartment. The man had been sitting two rows behind Danny. He wasn't sick. He just didn't want to sit next to a soldier. What kind of a world was Danny returning to?

CHRIS WAS IN bed asleep just past midnight. Danny walked into Chris' room with his walker and eased into his bed. Chris woke up, but didn't say anything. Danny lied down quietly. The light of the television illuminated the room.

"What ya' doing Dad?" Chris asked.

"I don't like it dark son, sorry." Danny replied.

"Ok, Dad. I got to get some rest, I have a long day tomorrow."

Chris closed his eyes. About thirty minutes later, Danny got out of the bed and walked with his walker to the bathroom.

Chris heard the water running in the tub. He got up and curiously watched from the hallway. Danny undressed and submerged himself under the water. He lay there half lifeless, running more hot water every few minutes.

"What's wrong Dad? It's after midnight. Why are you taking a bath?"

"I'm freezing to death son. My clothes are soaking wet. My legs and back ache so bad I can hardly stand it. I just need to soak in hot water. Can you get me some dry clothes?"

"Sure, Dad, I'll be in here if you need me."

Danny got out of the tub after about thirty minutes. He then came back to Chris's room and laid in the bed. Still restless, he flipped through the channels without any direction. He finally fell asleep. Shortly after, he woke up again, went back into the bathroom, and ran another tub of water.

Chris rolled over in the bed and sighed. Once again, he watched his dad closely. This routine went on all night long until day break. Danny would soak in the bath tub, then change into different clothes. Chris didn't sleep all night.

"THAT FLIGHT lasted forever!" thought Danny as he exited the airline ramp leading to the terminal in Cincinnati after a five-hour flight. He looked up at the board to find the gate for his connecting flight to Huntington, WV. It was late December, 1969 and he was one step closer to home.

Danny felt like he must be the most insidious creature to walk the earth for all the stares he received from the passing travelers in the hallway. "What did I do wrong?" thought Danny. "I just did my duty to keep us free."

He stopped by a little shop about one hundred feet from his departing gate. Danny walked up and looked at the menu. A petite girl, just past pimple age with dark blond hair, stood behind the counter with a towel in her hand. "What do you want?" she asked with the sternness of a hardened woman twice her age.

"Ah . . . I will take a . . ."

"Come on! Hurry up! I have some real customers to take care of."

Real customers? This was nuts! Somehow, Danny pinched his tongue and held back what he really wanted to say to her. Instead, he said, "I will just have a coffee."

As he walked towards the gate holding his coffee and duffle bag, he made a decision. He was done with flying for one very long day. He would find another way to get home. It wasn't the girl at the coffee shop, or even the man on the plane, that had changed his mind. It was . . . well, a promise. A promise he had already broken.

He was nervous about getting on that plane from Cincinnati to Huntington. While in Vietnam, Danny had witnessed many helicopters going down. He had been in one crash himself. Danny had promised himself that if he made it home, he would never fly again. He knew it was irrational, and that flying was safe, but how do you explain something logically to your emotions?

Danny made a decision. He had made it through Nam in one piece, and he wasn't going to risk the flight from Cincinnati to Huntington. He walked outside of the terminal and put up his hand to hail a cab. It was snowing and bitter cold. Something Danny hadn't seen or felt in several years.

Almost immediately, a cab pulled up to the curb. Danny stepped inside and said, "Greyhound Bus Station, please."

"Will do, G.I. Joe," said the cabbie.

With a sigh, Danny said, "Man, I just got back from 'Nam. I just want to get home."

"'Nam, huh? Tough war. Not many folks are for it," said the cabbie. "Where's home for you?" asks the driver as he sped towards the bus station.

"Huntington, West Virginia."

In a few minutes, Danny was at the bus station, buying his ticket. He boarded the bus and sat in the front row, right behind the driver. He couldn't relax. He was only one hundred and fifty miles from home, but felt fearful that he wouldn't make it.

CHAPTER THIRTEEN

TAKE ME HOME, COUNTRY ROADS

CHRIS CALLED DANNY'S LAWYER, MARK, THE next day and asked him if he could call the doctor and see what could be done with his dad. If things didn't change, Chris may have to put him in a controlled living facility. Maybe Mark could call the VA again or get a referral to a nursing home that had security.

Mark reviewed Danny's medical records and found that the doctors had Danny on eleven antipsychotic, anxiety, sleep and pain medications in the hospital. They were used to treat schizophrenia, bipolar disorder or manic depression. The side effects were aggressive behavior, agitation, anxiety, blurred vision, difficulty concentrating, difficulty speaking, loss of balance control, mask-like face, memory problems, restlessness, need to keep moving, and (severe) trouble sleeping. No wonder his dad was acting the way he was.

Chris and Mark sat down with Danny and told him the situation with the drugs. Even though Chris was his surrogate and could legally make that decision by himself, they wanted to talk to him. Danny listened and seemed to understand. When they asked him if he wanted to go off the drugs, he said: "I'll think about it."

Later, Danny walked into the office and looked at all his Marine medals from Vietnam. He read the two Purple Heart Citations of the missions he was on when he was wounded. He realized who he is, what he went through, and what he is made of. He is a Marine. . . and Marines always find a way.

Danny searched the house, found all of his prescriptions and flushed them down the toilet.

"It's you and me now, Lord." He prayed as he got down on his knees.

"Heavenly Father, I am here again at another crossroads of my life. I need your help Lord; I need your guidance now more than ever. I know you know all and I know you already know my fate. Lord, you have taken me through many life and death situations. You have kept me alive for a purpose. I pray that you cure me of my illness and get me back on the road to the purpose you gave me. I need a sign to help lead the way. In Jesus name I pray, Amen."

Danny looked out the window into the dark, cool night. He grabbed a cane, put on his coat and went outside. He slowly made his way down the sidewalk towards the nearby railroad tracks.

The lights of the parking lot illuminated the tracks. Danny made his way onto the gravel walkway beside the tracks, and walked a short distance looking around for the area the homeless live.

"Hey, you looking for something pal?" A drifter asked.

Danny focused in on a dark figure coming out of the dark.

"If you're looking for drugs, we don't have any mister."

"I'm not looking for drugs. I'm looking for a guy that saved my life a month ago."

"I was told he pushed me off the track just before an Amtrak ran over me."

"You know anything about him?"

"So, you're that crazy S-O-B that was ready to end it all huh?" The drifter replied.

"I'm a veteran; I was having some issues. I'm not sure what I was trying to do. Did you see what happened?"

"No, we just heard about it from Michael. He told us you were looking straight into the lights of the Amtrak and waiting for it to run over you. He pushed you out of the way just in time."

"Where is Michael? I want to thank him for saving my life."

"Mister, he left here as fast as he came. We have never seen him before, and haven't seen him since. He was a drifter, a rail rider, a hobo."

"Do you know his last name?"

"No. Sorry."

In the near distance, a train horn is blaring. A fast approaching locomotive is approaching. The lights of the oncoming train penetrate Danny's eyes.

Danny stepped onto the track and stared at the train as it bore down on him. The conductor blew the emergency whistle.

"Hey man, you're not going to do that crazy sh*t again are you?" The drifter asked.

"It will be ok." Danny responded calmly.

"Man, you're crazy!" The drifter screamed as he ran away.

Danny waited until the train was close, and then moved off of the track. The train sped on by, just like Danny's life had the past month.

As he watched the speeding train go by, his cell phone ringing broke his thoughts.

He let it ring several times before finally opening the line. On the other end was Chris.

"Dad! Dad! Are you there? Where the h*ll are you Dad?! Dad, answer me! You're driving me crazy!" Chris screams.

"What is that noise, Dad? Are you on the railroad track?"

Danny smiled and terminated the call without answering Chris.

He looked up and down the railroad track and realized what could have happened if a mysterious drifter or guardian angel hadn't been there a month ago to save him.

IT WAS LATE, 11:00 PM on the night of December 27th, 1969, after a long, four-hour ride on snowy roads, the Greyhound Bus pulled into the terminal in Huntington. Danny carefully stepped off the bus and set his feet on the ground he didn't think he would ever feel again. There was something about being home; no ground ever felt so solid or secure.

Danny walked several blocks and checked into the old Prichard Hotel in downtown Huntington. It was now a dump, but it was all he could afford. He put his duffle on the bed, then pushed down on it to check the comfort level of the springs. Danny figured it would be about as comfortable as sleeping on an ammo box. Oh well, at least he didn't have to worry about a night raid by the Viet Cong.

After a few minutes of nothing, Danny decided to go out and get some air. Still in his winter dress Marine uniform, he headed off down the street. At first, he was going nowhere in particular, but then he thought of the Sea Breeze nightclub. It was on the same street as the Prichard. Danny had played many gigs there with his old band. His mind went to pleasant memories of twirling his drumsticks between his fingers as he sat behind his old set of skins.

Outside the club, Danny rang the bell and the bouncer immediately opened the door. Danny smiled when he saw it was Harry. Harry was a big man — really, he was overweight. But those extra rolls of cushion just made him more intimidating as a bouncer, kind of like an irritated bulldog.

As soon as Harry saw him, he enveloped Danny in a big bear hug. "Danny Lane! Where the h*ll have you been? We thought you were dead. No one has heard from you in almost two years. Man, what happened to you? You look like a skeleton."

"Nah, the commies couldn't kill my sorry butt, they just made me go on a diet," laughed Danny. "Seriously, I didn't think I would come back from 'Nam alive, so I figured, why bother people?"

"Well, it is great to see you, Danny. Come on in! The first beer is on me."

"Wow, I should go to war more often if you're buying."

As Danny made his way to the bar, he noticed that some of the members of his old band were on stage. He nodded to them as he sat down on a stool.

Harry bounded right up on stage, grabbed the mic, and announced, "Attention, all you drunks! My good friend, Danny Lane, is home from Vietnam. Let's party!"

The bar erupted into cheers and whistles. Danny gave the crowd a little wave. It felt good. He was finally getting his *welcome home*.

After a few minutes — and a few beers — the lead guitar player, Ray, called to Danny from the stage, "Sit in with us, Danny. The skins are waiting for you. It will be just like the old days."

Standing up, Danny asked, "Cool, man. What's the next song?"

"*Devil with the Blue Dress On*, by Mitch Rider and the Detroit Wheels"

"Yeah, alright, I love that song."

Minutes passed like seconds, as Danny allowed the rhythm of the music to flow through his hands and into the drumsticks. Who knows how many rock songs he played that night, but he didn't care, because he hadn't felt this good in a very long time.

After a rewarding night, Danny walked back to the Prichard and got a restful night's sleep. For a while, the nightmare of his past and his fear of the future faded away into slumbering bliss. The future could wait till tomorrow.

Danny called his friend, Steve Newman. They had discussed Danny buying Steve's 1965 Chevy Impala SS if he made it back from the war. Steve agreed, and Danny took him the hard-earned cash from his twenty-four-hour-a-day job as a soldier in Vietnam. Danny loved that car. It could literally fly.

In his Chevy hot rod, Danny went to visit his good friend Darrell. He was now married and expecting a child. After a wonderful visit, Danny drove the 30 miles to Sidney, WV to visit his grandmother, Nola, who had raised him.

Nola, who Danny called "Mom," and her husband Lindsey Sr., who Danny called "Dad," lived off a country road on a peaceful property that was a little bit of heaven. As Danny pulled into the driveway and parked the car, he paused and took in the good feelings of childhood and love.

He noticed Mom looking out the front door. Nola was in her mid-sixties now, with salt and pepper hair that she always wore up in a bun. Danny hurried out of the car and Mom hurried out the front door. Her long country dress flowed behind her as she ran. They hugged in an embrace that stopped time, or Danny at least wanted it to.

Nola than looked at her grandson and said, "Let me look at you. Danny Boy, you are so skinny. What happened to you?"

"I know, Mom. I have been sick. I got malaria over there."

"Why didn't you write me from the war? I have been worried sick."

Danny looked down at the ground, then lifted his head and looked into the love of his grandmother's eyes, "I really didn't write anyone while I was over there. I wrote Judy once, and I wrote Darrell. I didn't think I would make it back, and I didn't think anyone really cared."

"Danny, you listen to me and you listen good. I have always loved you. You are like my son, and a mother never stops worrying about her kids."

"I am sorry, Mom. I didn't mean to worry you. I wanted to come see you and tell you how much I appreciated you raising me and taking care of me. If it wasn't for you, I don't know what I would have done."

"Danny, you have always been a blessing. I considered it a great honor and privilege to raise you. Judy had to work, and I didn't mind raising you. Now, let's go get you some of my famous sausage gravy and biscuits. I have got to fatten you up."

As Danny was enjoying a breakfast he thought he would never have again, Nola asked, "Danny, what did happen to you over in Vietnam?"

"Mom, I would rather not talk about it. It was a nightmare. I'm home in one piece, and that's all that matters."

"Ok. Here, let me get you some more food," Nola said, as she filled Danny's plate full of another helping of country heaven. "I remember a number of years ago, around Thanksgiving time, when you were coming home from school. When you didn't show up, I went to look for you and found you crawling on the road. When I got to you, you were having trouble breathing. That was the most scared I have ever been in my life."

"For what seemed like forever," she continued, "the doctors did not know what it was. We were told it could be polio or leukemia. We thought we would lose you. Do you remember that? Your legs were paralyzed for a year."

"Yeah, I remember, Mom. I had to learn to walk all over again."

"You didn't start getting better until the doctors discovered it was a rare strain of Rheumatic Fever. Those were hard days. Looking at you now, you look as skinny as you did back then. Are you sure you are ok? Should we get the doctor to look at you?"

"Really, I am ok, Mom. The Marine doctors checked me out." Changing the subject quickly, Danny blurted out. "I know what I want to do now, Mom. I want to be a cop like Oliver. They gave me his revolver after he died. I want to wear his gun when I become a cop, in memory of him."

"Well, that sounds fine, Danny Boy. But first, you have to fatten up. Keep eating!"

"How are Larry and Bubby doing?" Danny asked. Larry and Bubby were Nola's sons that Danny was raised with. Larry and Danny were three years apart in age and like brothers.

"They are fine. Larry is still a police officer in Cleveland, Ohio and Bubby is working construction. He will be home in a few hours." Nola answered.

"I remember when Larry and I were kids and played in the sandbox with those little green, plastic, Army men you bought us. Who would know then that both of us would become soldiers." Danny added.

"I suppose God did son. I suppose God did." Nola answered. In deep thought, Danny smiled at his grandma and nodded.

Danny hated to leave the warm love of his Mom, but he now realized that her love was with him wherever he went. As he drove off on that cold, fall day, he thought about his future — it looked bright.

Danny contacted some of Oliver's friends at the Huntington Police Department. They had known Danny since he was a child. They encouraged him to apply for a job as a police officer when he turned twenty-one years old. For Danny, that big day would happen in a few weeks.

In late December, Danny drove to Cleveland to pay his respects to the Greek's parents and his girlfriend Sophia. It was a long, five-hour drive in snowy weather. In the back seat of his car, Danny had loaded Sotere's personal belongings that he kept and brought home from Vietnam. He hoped that these few items would bring comfort to the Greek's family.

Danny dreaded the moment he would see Sotere's family, particularly Sophia. What can you say in such a moment? There are surely no words that can ease their pain. Danny was feeling the pain of mourning himself.

After he double-checked the address on the front of the envelope, Danny pulled up and parked on the street in a quiet neighborhood in Parma, Ohio. Sure enough, this was the place: Sophia's house. The address was found on the envelope of one of Sophia's letters to Sotere. Danny was sure that Sotere had read the one in his hand many, many times.

"Well," Danny thought, "I need to get this over with." He slowly opened the car door and walked up the sidewalk leading to the door. After a couple of minutes, he mustered up the courage and knocked.

The door slowly opened, and the beautiful Greek girl that Danny had seen in the pictures stood before him. As their eyes met, it was like they had known each other for years. "Hello, Sophia?" Danny asked.

"Yes, I am Sophia," she answered.

"My name is Danny Lane. I served in Vietnam with the Greek . . . I mean, Sotere."

"Yes, I know. I have seen many pictures of you."

"Oh."

"Sotere sent me rolls of film to develop for him when he was in Vietnam. He always talked about you in his many letters. Please come in."

"Sophia, I just got back from over there, and I have these letters that you wrote to him. He would have wanted you to have them."

Puzzled, Sophia asked, "What do you mean, Danny?"

"Sophia, I am so sorry. I know the loss I feel can't compare to what you must be feeling. Sotere was my best friend . . . he was such a brave soldier. You would have been so proud of him."

"Danny, what are you talking about?"

Tears formed in the corners of Danny's eyes. "About Sotere's death. I . . . just wanted . . . you to know how I felt . . ."

Before Danny could continue, Sophia blurted out, "Danny! Sotere is NOT dead! He is alive!"

"What? He's alive? How? I talked with the Marines who saw it happen. They said he was killed."

"Danny, I don't know. Sotere's parents had been told he was dead too. Then a few days later they were told he was alive and in critical condition in the hospital in Tokyo."

Danny instinctively reached out and embraced Sophia. Now the tears flowed freely down both their cheeks. Danny wiped his face and asked, "Where is he now? Is he still in Japan?"

Sophia broke into a beautiful smile. "No, he is in the bedroom."

"What!? He is here? Can I see him?"

As the words exited Danny's mouth, footsteps were heard coming down the hallway. "Sophia, dear, is someone here?" came a familiar voice Danny thought he would never here again.

Danny's and Sotere's eyes met as Sotere reached the end of the short hallway. As he leaned on a wooden cane, Sotere said, "Dan Bo, what the h*ll? What are you doing here?"

Danny ran across the room and grabbed his brother. "I thought you were dead, Greek!"

With a sly smile, Sotere said, "You know me, Dan Bo. Those commies could never kill me. I had to get home so Sophia and I could get married."

"What? You two are married?"

"Yeah. Last month."

"Congratulations! To both of you," Danny said, glancing back at Sophia. He turned back to Sotere. "What happened? The guys in Kilo Company said you were killed. They even said your body fell off the helicopter as they loaded you on board."

"What? I don't remember any of that. In fact, I don't remember anything after I got shot. We were getting hit hard and I was returning fire... then, I remember a sharp pain in my back. I woke up in Japan. I was told later that I got shot in the back, and an RPG B-40 rocket got me, Combat, and Wells. When I woke up, Combat was in the bed next to me."

"Is Combat going to be ok?"

"Yeah, he just had some shrapnel. It was his third Purple Heart, so he got shipped back home before I did."

"What about Wells?"

"I don't know if he made it or not," said Sotere. "We will have to look into that."

Looking down at the cane, Danny said, "Tell me about your wounds. You are on a cane. Are you going to be ok?"

"Yeah. I am going to be fine, Dan Bo. Like I said, those gooks couldn't kill me. All they could do was give me a little R&R."

"You know, I thought you were dead since September 8th. I even cried when I heard."

"I didn't know you cared so much, Dan Bo," said Sotere, lightening the mood.

"I spent three months in the bush without you, Combat, and Wells. It was awful! I almost didn't make it back, even on the last day."

"Well, we are both here my friend. That is all that matters."

They sat in the living room and talked hours about everything. It was the best feeling Danny had in a very long time. "What are you going to do now, Greek?"

"I'm going to work with my brother in the garbage collection business. We have our family business here in Parma, Ohio. It is called Karas & Karas. I will help him run the company. What are you going to do?"

"I am going to be a Cop. I start in a few weeks."

With a chuckle, Sotere said, "So, you're still trying to save the world, huh, Dan Bo?"

"Yeah . . . I'm just getting started!"

EPILOGUE

For Danny Lane, the journey he walked in *Some Gave It All* was a beginning point for him in many ways.

Danny was discharged from the hospital with very little hope of recovering and was left to deal with his medical condition on his own. For Danny, his battle to conquer his health issues almost forty years after Vietnam were as dark and dangerous as the jungle itself. Danny is a fighter, so he committed himself to the battlefield again — this time with himself and his future. He had much to live for and still much to accomplish. Danny began training like the World Champion and Martial Arts Master that he had once been. He began lifting weights, running, and knocking the cobwebs off his martial arts skills. Determined to become a Master again, he kept one goal in his mind: to travel and teach martial arts seminars again.

It was hard work, but after a year and a half and with the grace of God, Danny's health continued to improve. He regained his mastery of the martial arts and got back to being a defense investigator, taking on high profile criminal cases. Little did he know that the best was yet to come — God led Danny to Gina Michelle Kelsey. It was a fairytale romance of God's making and love at first sight. They are the love of each other's lives and are happily married. Today, the Lanes live in Kentucky.

In 2015, I met Danny Lane. I was looking for a martial arts instructor, and my search led me to Danny. He began to take me under his wing and train me in the art of Tang Soo Do and the Chuck Norris System. In the process, we became fast friends.

As we talked and got to know each other, I knew he had a story that had to be told. Much more from the encouragement of Gina than myself, he agreed to the literary adventure, and we became writing partners. I knew what I was asking of him was not easy. I was asking him to go back in his memory and relive experiences that he had tried to forget for forty years. But, I knew his story of survival would help many with their challenges. And, Gina knew that it would help Danny conquer his PTSD.

Danny is one of my heroes. What he conquered forty-seven years ago in a jungle in Southeast Asia is the stuff that births legends. But, what he conquered to write this book with me is the stuff of heroes.

As for the rest of Fire Team #1, Sotere (The Greek), is a retired, successful businessman in Cleveland and is still married to his lifelong love Sophia. Many of the pictures in this book were taken by Sotere on the frontlines of Vietnam. He sent the rolls of film back home to Sophia for safe keeping.

Wells and Combat are alive and doing well, outside of medical issues. Unfortunately, many of their other squad members who made it home have since passed away.

Danny continues to make personal appearances and teach seminars around the world. He is regarded as one of the leading experts in combat tactics and self-defense. He just finished a book and video series with former CIA officer Jason Hanson called *Spy Combative Tactics* in addition to writing this book. He believes that telling this story was part of why God kept him alive. Danny's goal is to help veterans like himself tell their stories and help them recover from the atrocities of war.

Danny, Gina, Sotere and Sophia

Danny and "The Greek"

Danny returns fire at the NVA on Operation Meade River

Danny & The Greek prepare for an NVA attack near Laos

3/5 humping into "Dodge City" for a showdown with the NVA

The Greek needs a smoke after a firefight in the village

Danny ready to engage the NVA near Laos coming down
the Ho Chi Minh Trail

Nothing more dangerous than angry nineteen year old Marines

The Greek Flag also flies during combat

Danny and his Squad during some down time

SOME GAVE IT ALL

"Through the Fire" In the Vietnam War

Vietnam 1965 - 1971

**Special Dedications to PFC Nick Carangio,
Sgt. "Freddy" Gonzalez, Gunnery Sgt. John Canley
& Captain Gordon D. Batcheller**

The Battle for Hue — History's Four Missing Days

In 1968, I had the honor and privilege to be an eyewitness to military history. There are very few individuals who had the opportunity to observe *two* **Medal of Honor** recipients doing their thing up close and personal. It's taken 49 years to complete the narrative on what happened at Hue City during the 68 TET offensive; History's Four Missing Days.

On 31 January 1968, half of Alpha Company, First Marines was airlifted to Phu Bai from Quang Tri Vietnam. We were an undersized rifle company who hadn't bathed or ate hot chow in

SOME GAVE IT ALL | 223

three months. Many of us had dysentery, parasites in our belly, jungle rot and smelled like water buffalo dung. Phu Bai was going to be our Club Med with powdered eggs, cold showers and even some warm beer. Sometime after midnight, we were ordered to "saddle up" and board trucks. Our CO, Captain Gordon Batcheller informed us, "We're gonna help some CAG unit down the road; we'll be back by noon."

Most of us never made it back to Phu Bai. We were 150 mud Marines and awaiting us in Hue City were 10,000 NVA soldiers (*). Pretty shitty odds, *even* for Marines. A few clicks from the city proper we were attacked by mortars, rockets and automatic weapons. One Marine lay wounded on Highway 1, and Captain Batcheller ran into the killing zone and shielded the Marine with his body while returning fire. Four AK 47 rounds hit the Skipper, and my first thought was, "no way does he survive." Captain Batcheller *did* survive and was awarded the Navy Cross, but his wounds have hobbled him for the past 49 years. Somehow, three of us dragged and carried Batcheller to safety, and during the process PFC Ragusa was hit in the leg with an AK round. He buckled but maintained his balance. "You OK?" I asked. Ragusa nodded and somehow kept himself erect. Our remaining officers were back in Quang Tri, so Gunnery Sgt. John Canley took command and his XO by default was an E-5 Sgt., Alfredo Gonzalez.

We pushed north along Highway 1 toward Hue city with intermittent sniper and automatic weapons fire from our west. There was a three-foot muddy ditch that we used for cover and concealment. On the outskirts of the city, enemy rockets, mortar and machine gun fire hit us from the north. We were now in a deadly crossfire. An open rice paddy was east, and the enemy had cut off any retreat *south* back to Phu Bai. Winston Churchill said, "When you're going through hell, you keep on going." Gunny Canley, Alfredo Gonzalez, Nick Carangio and a few other Marines did just that. Under intense enemy fire, they ran into that open rice paddy and maneuvered themselves into position and eliminated the machine gun positions with hand grenades, LAW rockets, and M-16's. Had they not done so, most of the Alpha Company may have been wiped out.

I was with the first Alpha Company fire team that entered Hue city proper on 31 January, 1968. (**) The silence was deafening, and my first thought was that the worst was over. Little did I know that it would get worse —*much* worse. Over the next 3 days, I witnessed acts of bravery that never made it to any official documents. Most Alpha Marines had shrapnel wounds but refused medivac. One Marine with a bullet hole in his leg used his M-16 as a makeshift crutch. Canley, Gonzalez and Carangio distinguished themselves on a continuous basis. On 4 February, Sgt. Gonzalez made several individual attacks on an NVA fortified position, the St. Joan of Arc School. An NVA rocket-propelled grenade (RPG) ended his life and he was awarded the Congressional Medal of Honor. PFC Carangio exposed himself to heavy NVA fire while firing an M-60 machine gun in the off-hand position (see photo above). Gunny Canley rescued ten wounded Marines during those four days, and in every case, did so under intense enemy fire. I witnessed and assisted the Gunny in carrying and dragging many wounded Golf 2/5 Marines from the An Cuu bridge as they made their assault across the Perfume River. At the St. Joan of Arc school, Gunny Canley dropped a satchel charge of explosives on a company of NVA soldiers who were determined to hold that building at any cost. They sustained heavy casualties and retreated from the Saint Joan of Arc school.

I was fortunate to experience those four days in 1968. We lost many good Marines, and many more carry physical and mental scars to this day. Only 7 Alpha Marines who entered that city on 31 January left unbloodied some 31 days later. As of this writing, Gunny Canley was approved for the Medal of Honor 49 years later, and is awaiting the ceremony. The Gunny had initially been awarded the Navy Cross for his actions *after* 3 February, but not one word was documented for the missing four days from 31 January till 3 February. His heroism would have been lost forever were it not for the Alpha Company Marines who chronicled their observations almost 5 decades later. I'd like to thank Ray Smith, Eddie "Alfie" Neas, the late Jimmy Sullivan, Pat Fraleigh, "Buzzard" Watkins, "Buck" Stubbs, Bill Purcell, Pat Patterson, the late Nick Carangio, Gordon Batcheller, and Larry Bilby for this.

I once said that, "The most ferocious fighting machine the world has ever seen is a pissed off 19-year-old Marine." Looking back at the TET offensive, these words were equally as true in 1968 as they were in 1775, and, as they are today.

SEMPER FI DEVIL DOGS

John Ligato

John Ligato is a retired FBI agent who spent 8 years in deep cover with the Italian Mafia. He received three Purple Hearts in Vietnam and currently writes books. His latest book, *The Near Enemy,* on lone wolf terrorist (Amazon or Simon and Schuster) is his third novel.

(*) The number "10,000 NVA soldiers" was verified and documented in the American Hero Channel documentary titled, *Against The Odds – The Marines at Hue.*

(**) There has been much discussion on which unit made the *initial* entry into Hue' City on 31, January 1968. In fact, several books have mistakenly cited other units, but, Marine Corps historians have documented that Alpha Company 1/1 made the initial entry. (See above comment on *Against the Odds – The Marines at Hue.*)

John Ligato — 1967

John Ligato — 2014 at the
Citadel in Hue City

John Ligato and Nick Carangio (standing) at
wall with M-60 machine gun

Hue City Vietnam — 3 February 1968

ACTS OF VALOR SPECIAL DEDICATION

Captain Gordon D. Batcheller – Navy Cross

The President of the United States of America takes pleasure in presenting the Navy Cross to **Captain Gordon D. Batcheller** (MCSN: 0-80672), United States Marine Corps, for extraordinary heroism while serving as Commanding Officer, Company A, First Battalion, First Marines, FIRST Marine Division (Reinforced), Fleet Marine Force, in the Republic of Vietnam on 31 January 1986.

Elements of Company A were assigned the mission of reinforcing a unit of the Army of the Republic of Vietnam in the city of Hue. Joining a small armored column north of Phu Bai in Thua Thien Province, the unit proceeded along National Route One toward Hue.

On the southern edge of the city, the column was ambushed by a numerically superior enemy force using automatic weapons, mortars, recoilless rifles and B-40 rockets. Quickly organizing his outnumbered forces into a defensive perimeter and unmindful of the danger, Captain Batcheller boldly began directing his unit's return fire. Exhibiting sound tactical judgment and calm presence of mind under enemy fire, he formulated a plan of attack and courageously exposed himself to the intense enemy barrage as he began shifting his men to more advantageous positions from which they delivered accurate suppressive fire against the hostile emplacements. Although injured by fragments of an exploding enemy rocket round, he aggressively led his men in a fierce assault against the enemy blocking positions, steadfastly advancing until he reached a besieged Popular Force compound. As the enemy increased the intensity of their attack, one of the Marine tanks was hit by hostile automatic weapons fire and B-40 rockets, which wounded several of the crew members. Ignoring the danger from enemy rounds exploding all around him, Captain Batcheller unhesitatingly moved to the damaged vehicle to assist in removing the casualties. Simultaneously, he reorganized his force and succeeded in routing the enemy from its fortified positions. As the intensity of enemy fire to the front lessened, the column began receiving heavy automatic weapons fire from both flanks, seriously wounding Captain Batcheller in both legs. Exhibiting great courage and physical stamina, he supported himself with his elbows and resolutely continued to direct his men in repulsing the enemy until, weakened by the loss of blood from his serious injuries, his voice fell to a whisper. Even then, he bravely encouraged those near him as he lay receiving medical treatment. As a result of his determined efforts, National Route One was reopened, enabling the reaction force to reach the embattled city of Hue. By his exceptional heroism, outstanding tactical ability and steadfast devotion to duty at great personal risk, Captain Batcheller upheld the highest traditions of the Marine Corps and the United States Naval Service.

Richard M. Nixon
President of the United States

Gunnery Sergeant James L. Canley – Medal of Honor

The President of the United States of America takes pleasure in presenting the Medal of Honor to **Gunnery Sergeant James L. Canley** (MCSN: 1455946), United States Marine Corps, for extraordinary heroism while serving as Company Gunnery Sergeant of Company A, First Battalion, First Marines, FIRST Marine Division (Reinforced), Fleet Marine Force, during operations against the enemy in the Republic of Vietnam from 31 January to 6 February 1968.

On 31 January, when his company came under a heavy volume of enemy fire near the city of Hue, Gunnery Sergeant Canley rushed across the fire-swept terrain and carried several wounded Marines to safety. Later, with the company commander seriously wounded, Gunnery Sergeant Canley assumed command and immediately reorganized his scattered Marines, moving from one group to another to advise and encourage his men. Although sustaining shrapnel wounds during this period, he nonetheless established a base of fire which subsequently allowed the company to break through the enemy strongpoint. Retaining command of the company for the following three days, Gunnery Sergeant Canley on 4 February led his men into an enemy-occupied building in Hue. Despite fierce enemy resistance, he succeeded in gaining a position immediately above the enemy strongpoint and dropped a large satchel charge into the position, personally accounting for numerous enemy killed, and forcing the others to vacate the building. On 6 February, when his unit sustained numerous casualties while attempting to capture a government building, Gunnery Sergeant Canley lent words of encouragement to his men and exhorted them to greater efforts as they drove the enemy from its fortified emplacement. Although wounded once again during this action, on two occasions he leaped a wall in full view of the enemy, picked up casualties, and carried them to covered positions. By his dynamic leadership, courage, and selfless dedication, Gunnery Sergeant Canley contributed greatly to the accomplishment of his company's mission and upheld the highest traditions of the Marine Corps and of the United States Naval Service.

Richard M. Nixon
President of the United States

Sergeant Alfredo Gonzalez – Medal of Honor

For conspicuous gallantry and intrepidity at the risk of his life above and beyond the call of duty while serving as Platoon Commander, Third Platoon, Company A, First Battalion. First

Marines, First Marine Division, in the Republic of Vietnam. On 31 January 1968, during the initial phase of Operation HUE CITY Sergeant Gonzales' unit was formed as a reaction force and deployed to Hue to relieve the pressure on the beleaguered city.

While moving by truck convoy along Route #1, near the village of Lang Van Lrong, the Marines received a heavy volume of enemy fire.

Sergeant Gonzalez aggressively maneuvered the Marines in his platoon and directed their fire until the area was cleared of snipers. Immediately after crossing a river south of Hue, the column was again hit by intense enemy fire. One of the Marines on top of a tank was wounded and fell to the ground in an exposed position. With complete disregard for his own safety, Sergeant Gonzalez ran through the fire-swept area to the assistance of his injured comrade. He lifted him up, and though receiving fragmentation wounds during the rescue, he carried the wounded Marine to a covered position for treatment. Due to the increased volume and accuracy of enemy fire from a fortified machine gun bunker on the side of the road, the company was temporarily halted. Realizing the gravity of the situation, Sergeant Gonzalez exposed himself to the enemy fire and moved his platoon along the east side of a bordering rice paddy to a dike directly across from the bunker. Though fully aware of the danger involved, he moved to the fire-swept road and destroyed the hostile position with grenades. Although seriously wounded again on 3 February, he steadfastly refused medical treatment and continued to supervise his men and lead the attack. On 4 February, the enemy had again pinned the company down, inflicting heavy casualties with automatic weapons and rocket fire. Sergeant Gonzalez, utilizing a number of light antitank assault weapons, fearlessly moved from position to position firing numerous rounds at the heavily fortified enemy emplacements. He successfully knocked out a rocket position and suppressed much of the enemy fire before falling mortally wounded. The heroism, courage, and dynamic leadership displayed by Sergeant Gonzalez reflected great credit upon himself and the Marine Corps and were in keeping with the highest traditions of the United States Naval Service. He gallantly gave his life for his country.

Richard M. Nixon
President of the United States

Special Dedication to PFC Gordon Dean Perry
Purple Heart Recipient

Gordon Dean Perry

Born: November 22, 1949 in Bradshaw, West Virginia

Died: May 30, 1969, Quang Nam Province, Vietnam on
    Operation Pipestone Canyon

Unit: 3rd Battalion, 5th Marines
United States Marine Corps

Awards: Purple Heart, Vietnam Campaign Medal, Vietnam Service Medal, Combat Action Ribbon and other awards for his service.

Gordon Dean Perry was born November 22, 1949, in Brad-shaw, West Virginia, to Mary Katherine Cook Perry and Everett Edward Perry Sr. He joined an older brother, Everett Edward Perry Jr. (Ed). Sisters Beverly (Perry) Fragale, Kathy (Perry) Westbrook and Kimberly Perry Groves would be born into the family in 1951, 1954, and 1961.

After graduation, Dean and his friends joined another important organization: the United States Marine Corps. Like his father, Everett Perry, a Marine during World War II, and his brother Ed, who was already in the Army, Dean would join the military. Ed Perry returned home in September, after Dean left for training in August. Ed wanted to extend his tour, with the intent of keeping Dean in the states, because the family didn't want Dean to go to Vietnam. Ed was willing to postpone his planned September wedding to do this, but Dean was determined to go. The Perry family remembers that their son and brother was honored to serve.

The Perry family remembers that Dean and his friends, Dan Barker, Meade Grow, and Robert Gallon, joined together, and left for Basic Infantry Training Services with the Marines in August 1968. Dan Barker wrote that they all spent boot camp at Camp Pendleton. They were in infantry training together, but were separated during their specialty training. Dean and another friend, Joe Slavensky, went to specialized training as mortar men, while Dan Barker went into anti-tank assessment training. Meade Grow and Robert Gallon went to machine gun training. After boot camp, they went home to Morgantown for 30 days and then returned to the Marines to begin a 30-day staging period before going to Vietnam.

Pfc. Gordon Dean Perry became a member of the 3rd Battalion, 5th Marines, 1st Marine Division as an infantryman. He was assigned to Corporal Danny Lane's First Squad which had three fire teams and twelve men. On May 26, 1969 Operation Pipestone

Canyon commenced. It was 5 AM, the sun was not even beginning to poke up on the distant horizon. The ground shuttered under the pressure of heavy bombardment. Operation Pipestone Canyon was commencing with a blistering bombardment of the Area of Operation of the western region. The Naval ship the USS Newport News sat offshore and launched heavy 8-inch (203mm) shells one after another. Air Force B-52's saturated the AO (Area of Operation) in preparation for the invasion.

For the next four days and nights more than a *1000* Marines walked and fought their way towards "Dodge City". They took heavy causalities from small arms and bobby traps set along the way. Their mission was to secure a main railroad track area in "Dodge City" and set up blocking positions. Other American Marine, Korean Marines and the Vietnamese Army units were to sweep the Viet Cong towards them.

On the day of May 30th the Marines reached their objective and spent the day developing a perimeter and digging in.

Corporal Lane and his squad settled in an old cemetery. They dug in deep but not to disturb the deceased. They used the larger headstones as barriers to help stop the bullets and rocket attacks that knew would be coming. Sometime around midnight, an all-out assault erupts on their position. Danny, Gordon, Greek and another Marine named Combat returned fire. In the exchange of gunfire and rockets, Gordon got fatally hit while he was returning fire at the oncoming enemy. His actions were those of a true Marine hero who in the heat of battle stood his ground and gave his life fighting for other Marines and his country. His actions showed courage, bravery and fortitude beyond description. Corporal Lane was also wounded by rocket shrapnel.

Pfc. Gordon Dean Perry was buried in East Oak Grove Cemetery in Morgantown, West Virginia. Dean was one of the servicemen featured in the June 27, 1969, Life magazine cover story entitled "The Faces of the American Dead in Vietnam:

One Week's Toll." The feature story was about the 242 men who were killed between the dates of May 28 and June 3, 1969. Dean appears on page 28, looking fit and ready at the age of 19.

MARINE CORPS ACTS OF VALOR
Operation Meade River, Vietnam - November 20 - December 9, 1968

Operation Meade River was in its 19th day. From the beginning, it was a constant push to surround and eliminate a well-prepared and determined enemy, the NVA. At times, it felt like one continuous firefight with few intermissions. We had taken many casualties, but the enemy had taken many more. It was a contest of wills and determination. The evening of December 8 was no different. We knew there was a last pocket of resistance blocked by the river that would be difficult to take. We were ready as the evening approached and daylight turned to twilight, but so was the enemy. India Company got on line ready to defeat whatever or whomever was between us and the river, as we prepared to bring the operation to a close. As twilight turned to darkness, India Company pushed forward for our final drive toward the enemy. We probably moved forward less than 100 meters before the waiting and prepared NVA, with seemingly nothing to lose, lit up almost the entire company front with automatic weapons.

SSGT KARL TAYLOR MEDAL OF HONOR RECIPIENT

We responded, but the NVA brought us to a screeching halt. Casualties were many and immediate throughout most of the company. There was little cover to hide behind. Most platoons and the company headquarters suffered severely with dead and wounded Marines. Only Second Platoon on the right flank did not get exposed as severely. The heroism of many of our Marines kicked into action. Paramount in our minds was to retrieve the wounded as quickly as we possibly could. Marines continually exposed themselves to the automatic weapons fire to help their wounded brothers.

Heroes, like SSgt Karl Taylor (posthumously awarded the MOH), continually moved forward repeatedly to retrieve wounded Marines. In spite of multiple injuries, he saved several Marines until he succumbed to his wounds and took his last breath. 2ndLt Chris Tibbs was the Second Platoon

Commander. I was the Second Platoon Sergeant. Although Second Platoon received significant fire from the enemy, we did not have any serious injuries. Every other Platoon suffered significantly. Lt Tibbs and I coordinated and sent each of our three squads to help retrieve the dead and wounded from the other platoons that had fallen in front of the company's makeshift perimeter. The effort lasted all night. Time was critical in retrieving the wounded, since the enemy also moved forward during the night to ensure that any Marine they found wounded and alive was shot in the head. One or two wounded Marines who we couldn't get to because we did not know of their locations, were able to feign being dead and not get shot, as we discovered the following morning. My main thought throughout the night was to keep our Marines in the game. I did not want them to lose focus or succumb to fear or emotions. The tempo was high. Emotions were through the roof. Fear is contagious. I did my best to keep their heads on the mission at hand, on survival.

Daylight came and the fear and emotions subsided. We knew this day was the end of Operation Meade River. In our eagerness to get ready in the morning, we had overlooked one bunker with occupants. One of our Marines, who was part Native American and was an excellent tracker and observer, felt he smelled something and may have seen movement in the nearby bush. I immediately took off my pack and moved in the direction of where he thought he saw movement. Once inside the bush, I spotted a freshly dug fighting hole. I approached the fighting hole and engaged the two occupants inside with a pistol. Those were the last shots fired during Operation Meade River. The helicopters scheduled to transport us to the rear were circling overhead. Morale was picking up. We had just gone through the most hellish night of my 10 months in Vietnam. We lost many Marines that night. That night will forever be burnt into my memory.

Respectfully and Semper Fi,
F. Phil Torres
Colonel, U. S. Marine Corps, Retired
(Formerly Cpl Torres, Second Platoon Sergeant,
India Company, 3/26)

SILVER STAR RECIPIENT

SPECIAL DEDICATION TO PFC DANIEL BRUCE
Medal of Honor Recipient

Daniel D. Bruce

Born: May 18, 1950, Michigan City, IN

Died: March 1, 1969, Quang Nam Province, Vietnam

Unit: 3rd Battalion, 5th Marines

United States Marine Corps

Awards: Medal of Honor, Purple Heart, Vietnam Campaign Medal, Vietnam Service Medal, Combat Action Ribbon and other awards for his service.

Daniel Bruce had been in Vietnam less than two months when he was tragically killed March 1, 1969 in combat at Fire Support Base Tomahawk, in the Quang Nam Province, during Operation Taylor Common. Operation Taylor Common commenced on December 7, 1968 and the 5th Marines were going into their third month of constant combat. The Marines were finally closing the noose on Base Area 122, an NVA and VC stronghold in the mountains of Quang Nam Province known as the "Arizona Territory". A showdown was inevitable.

On March 1, 1969, Daniel was on bunker watch when the enemy attacked the Marine perimeters. These kamikaze type tactics were common by the NVA. During the attack a satchel charge by an NVA sapper was thrown at his position. Not being one to run from danger, Daniel caught the satchel charge and pulled it into his body. Wanting to protect his fellow Marines, he ran from his position trying to put some distance between the satchel and his fellow Marines, who would have undoubtedly been killed had it gone off near them. When the satchel exploded seconds later, Bruce was killed instantly. PFC Bruce put meaning to the saying "Greater love hath no man than to give his life for another." He was only 18 years old.

On March 2, 1969, the day after Bruce sacrificed his life for his fellow Marines, his future to be wife, Carey, gave birth to his daughter, Stacey.

Private First Class Daniel D. Bruce United States Marine Corps for Service as Set Forth in the Following Citation:

For conspicuous gallantry and intrepidity at the risk of his life above and beyond the call of duty while serving as a Mortar Man with Headquarters and Service Company, Third Battalion, Fifth Marines, First Marine Division, against the enemy in the Republic of Vietnam. Early on the morning of March 1, 1969, Private First Class Bruce was on watch in his night defensive position at Fire Support Base Tomahawk in Quang Nam Province when he heard movements ahead of him. An enemy explosive charge was thrown toward his position and he reacted instantly, catching the device and shouting to alert his companions.

Realizing the danger to the adjacent position with its two occu-pants, Private First Class Bruce held the device to his body and attempted to carry it from the vicinity of the entrenched Marines. As he moved away, Private First Class Bruce's indomi-table courage, inspiring valor and selfless devotion to duty saved the lives of three of his fellow Marines and upheld the highest traditions of the Marine Corps and the United States Naval Ser-vice. He gallantly gave his life for his country.

Richard M. Nixon
President United States of America

ABOUT THE AUTHORS

Danny Lane is a highly decorated US Marine, serving in combat in Vietnam in 1968-1970. He received two Purple Hearts, the Marine Combat Action Medal and numerous other commendations. He is a retired Police Officer, certified International Police Defensive Tactics Instructor, and an expert in Police and Military Defensive Tactics. Danny co-authored *Spy Combat Tactics* with former CIA Agent Jason Hanson, and has twenty-nine self-defense training videos — all found on his website DannyLane.com. Danny still teaches defensive tactics to law enforcement, military and the public all around the world. Besides writing, he currently works high profile criminal, civil and domestic cases as a private investigator with his beautiful wife, Gina.

Mark Bowser has written several books and is one of the top business speakers in the United States. He has given seminars for many organizations including Southwest Airlines, United States Marine Corps, FedEx Logistics, Ford Motor Company, Kings Daughters Medical Center, Princeton University, Dell Computers, and many more. His books include *Sales Success* with the late Zig Ziglar, *Jesus, Take the Wheel, Unlocking the Champion Within*, and *Nehemiah on Leadership*. He lives in the Cincinnati area with his wife and kids. Mark can be reached at www.MarkBowser.com.

CPSIA information can be obtained
at www.ICGtesting.com
Printed in the USA
JSHW041340060521
14342JS00002B/2